The
Butterfly
Experience

The
Butterfly
Experience

How to transform your life from the inside out

KAREN WHITELAW-SMITH

WATKINS PUBLISHING
LONDON

This edition first published in the UK and USA in 2012 by
Watkins Publishing, Sixth Floor, Castle House,
75–76 Wells Street, London W1T 3QH

1 3 5 7 9 10 8 6 4 2

Design and typesetting by Paul Saunders

Printed and bound in China by Imago

British Library Cataloguing-in-Publication Data Available
Library of Congress Cataloging-in-Publication Data Available

ISBN: 978-1-78028-378-4

www.watkinspublishing.co.uk

Distributed in the USA and Canada by Sterling Publishing Co., Inc.
387 Park Avenue South, New York, NY 10016-8810

For information about custom editions, special sales, premium and
corporate purchases, please contact Sterling Special Sales
Department at 800-805-5489 or specialsales@sterlingpub.com

This book is dedicated to my loving father, John W. Syme,
who died on 25 October 1999 from prostate cancer.
A private man, whose hugely positive influence
and courage inspired this book.

Acknowledgments

I would like to thank my mum and late dad for all their help and support throughout my life. Their wisdom guided me toward my path.

I am forever grateful to my loving husband Gordon, my rock, and our children Iain, Jennifer and Calum (my butterflies) who have always given me their continued support.

Finally, my thanks to Anne Buhrmann for her pre-publisher editing, encouragement and friendship.

Author's note
All case histories in this book are true.

Contents

STAGE THREE · THE COCOON
Going Within   129

STAGE FOUR · THE BUTTERFLY
Learning to Fly   185

Foreword

I FIRST ENCOUNTERED THE remarkable work of Karen Whitelaw-Smith at a time when my father had been diagnosed with terminal cancer. The doctors said the outlook was bleak, but my father, as a doctor himself, saw things quite differently. He worked through his cancer and finally achieved remission, and I witnessed the wonderful part that Karen's professional help and healing techniques played in his recovery. She came into our lives like a butterfly, quite magically, and since then we have become close friends.

In 2010, after a particularly difficult time, I called on Karen's services myself. The Butterfly Experience proved to be not only a powerful healing tool but also an inspirational aid to success, as Karen's meditational expertise and focus exercises helped me in my weekly preparation for the hit TV talent show *Popstar to Operastar*. I went on to win the show and then to perform in my debut opera, *Carmen*, at London's O2 Arena, the youngest-ever performer to take on the lead role of the bullfighter Escamillo in a professional opera, in what became the biggest production of an opera in the UK. As I took to the stage with the Royal Philharmonic and 200 performers, ready for the final curtain call in front of 20,000 people, there was one person in the audience who had helped me immeasurably who wasn't beside me to take a bow – Karen. And like a butterfly she flitted silently in the dark beyond the lights ... I could feel her energy in the crowd. She is a magnetic, magnanimous person and a terrific, trusted professional.

Life is wonderful and so precious! Don't waste it worrying, procrastinating, being unhappy or feeling frustrated. You hold in your hands a powerful tool to help you heal your life, succeed in your career and your relationships and make a change for the better. I have experienced it first hand and know that the Butterfly Experience works and is one that we can all aspire to.

Expect miracles!

Darius Campbell

West End actor and platinum-selling singer-songwriter

Note to the Reader

THIS BOOK WAS WRITTEN for everyone who finds it difficult to accept change. I was once that person. After years of developing my own techniques and deciding to change my own life, I want to offer you the chance to change your life for the better. It's the mark of spiritual growth that we want to share what we've learned – we want everyone to profit, to share in the yield, to enjoy its fruits. Today I am in control of my life and my destiny. I know where I'm going. I understand my purpose. I'm here to help others find an easier path through life, to show them how to live a life of abundance.

There is no one this book would not benefit. But I've written it for YOU. It's intended to be both practical and inspirational. Each section will provide you with tried-and-tested techniques for self-relaxation, visualization, goal-setting and pure energy work. You'll benefit most by working through the book from beginning to end, committing to the exercises and practising the techniques as you go. This is not a programme you can cherry-pick your way through. It should be worked through in chronological order. Don't try to skip ahead. Or is that what you think life is all about – shortcuts?

I want you to get maximum benefit from the work and I want that benefit to start today! I want you to enjoy your life as much as I enjoy mine. If you are willing to commit to change then you're halfway there. Using my solutions, you'll be amazed how quickly life starts to turn around.

A word of caution

In the Butterfly Experience, not everyone makes it through to flight. Some of you will become glorious butterflies. Some will hold on to fear and stay stuck, living in emotional turmoil. This book is not a magic wand. The Butterfly Experience requires discipline. Spiritual discipline. It requires spiritual energy and belief. It's *believing* that makes magic happen.

You are a seeker. You may already have tried many courses, therapies and training. You may have wasted money and come up empty. My techniques are free. You can do them from home. I even give you a guarantee that they will work. All I ask is that you start to bring some discipline into your life; practise, practise, practise and you'll soon experience mind-blowing results.

There is a Butterfly Experience Journal at the back of this book, to enable you to record your personal journey of self discovery. Journaling will help you to keep a record of where you are and how far you have progressed.

Moth or butterfly? Which will you be?

It's time to transform your life from the inside out.

Butterfly Blessings!

Karen Whitelaw-Smith

Introduction

ALL MY LIFE I'VE BEEN drawn to butterflies. I love their variety, their colours, their delicate strength. I call them my "Butterfly Blessings". There's an old saying that butterflies are drawn to healers; they've sought me out all my life. As I was sitting recently in a packed auditorium, a beautiful monarch butterfly flew onto my shoulder. Inwardly, I asked it to fly to my hand. It stayed for quite some time, allowing me to stroke its wings. When I whispered that it was free to leave it flew off, though with some hesitation. The beautiful creature circled me for some time before disappearing.

The butterfly is the perfect symbol for this book; it represents hope, happiness and lightness of being. Butterflies inspire. They're a sign of faith released. So it's easy to forget that the butterfly's beauty comes at great *cost*. Throughout its life journey each butterfly undergoes profound transformations, survives many obstacles. In that sense we are like butterflies, constantly changing and growing. At times our lives, too, can seem full of unbearable hardship.

I've written *The Butterfly Experience* to tell you that it doesn't have to be that way. I want this book to give you the magic ingredient for a successful, happy life. We can access energy to help us. Part of that is belief; we have to *believe* that we can change. My techniques are designed to anchor that belief. That pure energy. Alignment with that pure energy releases our creativity and our potential for happiness. I call it pure, source, divine, universal energy – these terms all mean the same thing. Anything that blocks this energy is easily recognized because it causes us unhappiness and distress.

You only have to be open to admitting that you want to change, to learn new ideas in order to attract abundance into your life. To feel happiness and start to love life more. The Butterfly Experience is pure positive energy. I want you to start thinking differently, to be open to the Butterfly Experience in new ways.

The universe is full of unlimited energy that every single person can tap into. How do you do that? There are three steps to opening yourself up to this amazing natural resource:

1. **Change your mindset**. For now, you only need to be open to speaking more positively. You are training your mind to be still and to start to vibrate at a different energy frequency.

2. **Focus**. Simply by tuning into this energy frequency, you can start to attract more abundance into your life. By

focusing on what you want, you can draw it into your energy field.

3. **Practise self-relaxation**. This book contains some amazing techniques. You can start to envision how your life could be by deliberately letting go of tension and anxiety.

Why is it so important that we connect to that pure positive energy? Pure consciousness is our own spiritual essence. When you connect to that energy, you connect to yourself. When you practice self-relaxation, you open yourself up to an infinite possibility of opportunities. You begin to learn to still the mind and go within, to find out who you are.

When you are in alignment with that source energy you know how good it feels. You feel happy and excited, and experience pure joy. When you are out of alignment, you also know. Everything seems to go wrong.

You attract what is going on in your life at any given moment in time. There is no separation between you and your inner source, that pure God energy. You are one. Your life is influenced by all that is going on in and around you. The people, surroundings, thoughts and circumstances.

Many people live their lives in fear. But fear means you are out of alignment with that pure energy source. The ego kicks in and the inner voice tells you that you are not good enough. You become stressed. You push your body and burn out.

Simply by choosing to align with source energy you can really start to be free in your life. Only when you are connected to pure positive energy can you truly find peace and contentment.

My Butterfly Experience techniques will help you to overcome your fears, so you can finally be who you deserve to be. I want to help you to break out of your safe cocoon and experience personal freedom. I want you to stretch yourself, using the techniques and lessons that I've been living for many years. They are guaranteed to help you grow – *if* you are prepared to commit to change.

There are four stages in the Butterfly Experience. The first is the Egg stage, where you take a long hard look at yourself and find out who you really are – and what you really want. The second is the Caterpillar stage, where you will learn the amazing Butterfly Experience techniques and start to grow, gradually shedding everything that is keeping you from change. In the Cocoon stage, you take this process even further, voyaging within yourself to nurture the innate qualities of your authentic Self and complete the miracle of metamorphosis. (Of course, the butterfly pupa is technically termed a "chrysalis", but I like to use the word "cocoon", with all its associations of protection, warmth and inwardness.) Finally, in the Butterfly stage you learn to fly – and make your dreams a reality.

Just like the butterfly, you already have everything you need for the journey within you. You've begun a process that will lead you to a life of joy and abundance. These are no empty promises. They have become manifest in my life and in the lives of my clients. They can become real for you, too. This is *your* chance to fly. The Butterfly Experience will enhance and enrich your life in ways you can't even begin to imagine. If the monarch butterfly, a tiny, fragile creature, can fly thousands of miles to its winter resting place, what could you achieve?

I know some of you may be feeling sceptical. So here's a challenge. Read *The Butterfly Experience*. Apply the techniques for 30 days. Challenge them. Test them. And watch your life change. It's time. Time to be positive about what you want from life. Time to use your mind to achieve the results you need. Time to accept responsibility for your own happiness. Today's thoughts create your tomorrow. You *can* change. The Butterfly Experience has begun.

STAGE ONE · THE EGG

Finding Out Who You Are

CHAPTER ONE

_____

You Can Be a Butterfly

WAITING FOR THE MIRACLE that will make you happy? Fed up always looking to other people for approval? Or just wishing that your life had come with a set of instructions?

Well, now it does! Welcome to the Butterfly Experience! The book you're holding will give you the guidance you've been waiting for.

- It will show you how to take control of your destiny.

- It will teach you how to stop repeating the same mistakes time after time.

- It will help you make conscious choices that will lead you to success and happiness.

With proven ideas, techniques, tips and solutions, the Butterfly Experience is the key to a healthy, happy and abundant life.

You know that feeling when you want the world to stop so that you can get off and just *think*? The Butterfly Experience offers you that chance. Even better, it offers a new way of thinking about:

WHO you are

WHERE you're going, and

WHAT you want out of life.

Today is the day you quit bumbling along, and stop being swept up by other people's agendas.

To be truly happy you have to get to know the *truth of who you are.*

The closest most people get to being truly happy is daydreaming. Instead of focusing on what we want and how to get it, we make the classic mistake that guarantees we stay right where we are. We concentrate on what we *don't* want. By giving our energy to the negative we attract it. So we stumble at setbacks. We struggle at the mercy of our emotions. Above all we allow ourselves to feel like victims. There's tremendous power in that mindset – victims don't need to change. So negative thinking becomes an ingrained habit. Here's a heads-up:

Negative thinking harms us.

Negative thinking is the root cause of disease.

Negative thinking draws negative people and experiences into our lives.

Yet we *still* insist on doing it! So how do we stop being casualties of our own thinking? The real question is, "How motivated are you to *change?*"

> *Happiness is a butterfly, which when pursued is always just beyond your grasp, but which if you will sit down quietly, may alight upon you.*

NATHANIEL HAWTHORNE (1804–1864)

With a positive mindset we can achieve anything that we set out to do. But first we have to conquer the enemy within – our own negativity. If ignorance or fear has been your excuse up until now, here's a warning: they're officially no longer valid! It's time to get honest here. No more lies. No more self-deceit. The truth about who you are and what you want is about to become the springboard that will catapult you into the life you deserve.

Life is simple. Every new day presents us with choices and challenges. How we cope with them dictates the quality of our lives. The secret to success isn't elusive; we have to know what we want, work hard for it and persist when things get tough. Yet we keep on making the same mistakes, expecting a different outcome. We refuse to abandon the comfort of our old thinking – our cocoon – for fear of trying something new.

Change is coming

The procrastinating is over. That's just a big word for "fear". No one likes change, but without it, nothing changes. So open yourself up to this process, welcome it, embrace it. Follow the directions in this book and watch the magic happen.

Butterflies are quite different from all other creatures on the planet. To evolve, they undergo a series of profound, miraculous changes. The Butterfly Experience is all about change – why we need it, how to do it and how to make that process as painless and as enriching as possible. This book is full of meditations, creative exercises and positive, healing, new thinking that will awaken your inner spirit. The purpose of living is to be alive! I want you to live life consciously, and to be alive to its possibilities and wonders. At the end of this process I want you to rise majestically to the vibrant and unique life you deserve.

The butterfly emerges from its cocoon as a captivating, joyous creature. But this "flying flower" has transformed itself completely, going through four separate stages of change. Each stage has a different goal. Each has a different set of obstacles that must be overcome if the butterfly is to survive. Our lives – if they are to be lives worth living – undergo similar metamorphosis. Each phase of our journey should bring us closer to our goal. At each stage you have to believe that change is possible. You have to *believe* that you're entitled to happiness – that it's your birthright.

Fundamentally we're all the same – there is a universality of thoughts and emotions. But the standards and values that *you* bring to the Butterfly Experience are your unique gifts to this process. I want to help you to recognize them and learn to live by them always. Let's begin …

Find the real you

The first stage in the life cycle of the butterfly is the egg. Not the most glamorous of titles, I'll grant you, but it's our starting point. We humans start life as an egg. So the egg is the symbol of life and the greatest gift we ever receive.

The appropriate response to any gift – especially one so precious and fragile – is gratitude. And that's where I want you to begin. Reflect for a moment on your life. Consider all that you've been through, the lessons you've learned and the people who've helped you along the way. Take yourself back in your imagination, allow different circumstances to float into your subconscious. See the faces of your loved ones, your friends, the people who have taught you life's lessons (both beautiful and painful). Be grateful for the wisdom you have today.

Butterfly eggs – just like us – come in different colours, shapes and sizes. Each egg is laid in a protected place. Hopefully your family and friends provided that protection for you, allowing you to shelter from life's harms. If not, somehow you have survived and developed ways of coping. Similarly, each butterfly egg has a hard outer shell, which protects the new life inside. It's called the *chorion*. I like to think of it as the face or mask we develop, the false identity that shelters our egos. These protective mechanisms and behaviours can keep us from harm, but they can also limit us. Reading this book means you have a sense that your life should somehow be "more". All you need for this new beginning is the tiniest of cracks to appear in your protective outer shell. A tiny change in your thinking. A chink in your armour, just enough to let in new light.

Is it possible for you to admit that there may be more to learn? It's time to ask yourself: "Am I ready to really take control of my life?" If the answer is "Yes", you've hit the jackpot, because I'm here to give you a "how to". I'm going to teach you simple techniques that will help you to be happy and healthy, to have bundles of energy and to enjoy an overflow of abundance. It's time to get into the driving seat of your own life. Instead of being spoon-fed happiness, or taking it at someone else's expense, why not create it? Success is not a matter of luck – it's a reward.

Each new butterfly's life begins as an egg and depends for sustenance on what's already inside it. The same applies to us on our journeys. When the chips are down, all we have are our resources within. In the Butterfly Experience the first job is to identify those resources – your existing strengths, the unique qualities you possess, what's happening inside you today. The first stage of the Butterfly Experience will identify your untapped resources. This foundation will provide the wherewithal for you to grow, spiritually and emotionally.

Know your life's purpose

Of course the butterfly has it easier to a degree. It's following a predetermined path. In order for you to rise up, you'll need to find *your* path. So it's time to face facts: whenever life isn't going according to plan, it's because you don't *have* a plan! That's about to change. The Butterfly Experience is designed specifically to help you create an individual plan for your life.

Remember, this plan is for you and you alone. No more cobbling together ideas based on other people's ideas of contentment. No more worrying about the expectations of family or the needs of friends. You can do this for you, using my Butterfly Experience techniques. It's only by looking inside yourself, by becoming conscious of your own thoughts, that you can start to grow. Soon *you* will decide what to think and feel. *You* will decide what ideas to accept or reject. *You* will control your body. Most importantly, after the Butterfly Experience you'll never again wonder why you're here. I'm not talking about the job you have, or the relationship you're in. I'm talking about knowing the reason you *exist*.

As a child watching the moon landings I was struck by one detail in the coverage Neil Armstrong received – ever since childhood his dream had *always* been to walk on the moon. He *never* gave up on it. Armstrong fulfilled his ambition through determination and positive thinking.

Do you know your life's purpose? What was your reason for getting up this morning? If you're clear on these points, or if you've already found whatever it is that makes your heart sing, we're going to improve on that.

If you *don't* have a focus that drives your life, this book will help you to find it. If your purpose has been foisted upon you by other people or if you have "people-pleased" yourself right into misery, the Butterfly Experience will show you how to change that. The techniques you are about to learn are simple, yet all too few people use them. Why? Because they don't understand their *necessity*.

Each of us is in the process of building our life, so we need a solid, structured plan to follow. The Butterfly Experience will provide you with a guide, which, if adhered to, promises success.

Our experience starts with who we are today and shows us how we can get to where we want to be. Its ultimate aim is to help us fulfil our destiny. In order to feel fulfilled we need to know that we are making a difference. We need aims and goals so that we can grow to our full potential. Unless we are connected to the world in some joyous, fulfilling way, we cannot love ourselves as we should. Without self-love, our view of the world is tarnished. But when we learn to love ourselves, magic happens deep inside.

In his Nobel Prize acceptance speech, Dr Martin Luther King said that the most important ingredient for success was self-belief. We have to feel proud of who we are. Creating your Butterfly Experience Blueprint – the practical plan for realizing your dreams – will give your life *significance*. It will increase your sense of self-worth. This life plan will motivate you and boost your determination.

Using your Butterfly Experience Blueprint, you will set

out to do what's necessary and do it to the best of your ability. When the door of opportunity opens, this book and its *energy* will give you the courage to walk through. Pure energy is infectious.

Tapping into pure energy will help you to study harder, work harder and create solutions to problems as they occur. It will help you to get out of bad situations instead of hanging on, hoping they'll improve. Having a plan doesn't mean that we're immune to bad experiences, but when things do happen that are out of our control, your Butterfly Experience Blueprint will help you to make the right choices. It will hold you accountable. A Butterfly Experience Blueprint helps us to realize our strengths and work on our limitations. It helps us to understand that we fail only when we give up.

Be very clear – the Butterfly Experience is the key to your new life. You will become a new creature. My life has changed beyond recognition since I developed the techniques in this book. I have used them to change my thinking, so that now I live a life without limitations. Life is not a mystery or something to be feared, but a joyous journey.

Mapping out your path isn't difficult when you have the tools. The starting point is the same for all of us. It's our subconscious, our essence. Our pure energy. We are what we think. The subconscious mind never shuts down. Even when we're sleeping, it's busy processing our thoughts. So it stands to reason that we should try to understand it better.

CHAPTER TWO

Change Your Attitude

THIS BOOK'S PURPOSE is to get you thinking positively about your life. In the West we're just beginning to understand the value of positive thinking. Schools and businesses know how crucial it is to develop a positive culture. Even in my beloved home country, Scotland, where dourness and negativity are legendary, people are becoming increasingly aware of how positive thinking – and its opposite force – can shape our lives. Since childhood I have understood that my life and my destiny are controlled by my thoughts and I have used positive thinking to create the life I deserve.

I have *always* sent wishes out to the universe. This was something innate, untaught, which I've done automatically all my life. Fanatic about sports as a child, I regularly visualized myself running through the finishing tape and being awarded a gold medal. That vision became reality.

My visualization was so powerful it allowed me to back up my wish with action, always with an end goal in sight. Positive thinking has allowed me to raise a wonderful family, create amazing friendships, build two businesses and love myself for who I am. It has been the secret behind every success I have ever had – training with positive thinking leaders all over the world. It brought me my beautiful home, fashioned the relationships I have with my amazing husband and children. It is the source of my happiness.

We have to get rid of the idea that we are limited in what we can ask for. That belief system has to change. Our thinking is conditioned over the years by thoughtless comments from our parents, teachers, colleagues and others. But please remember that these limiting beliefs can be changed. You can change them NOW.

The conscious and the subconscious

Throughout our lives we are learning constantly. Experiences and emotions are stored in our minds, just like data on a computer, though of course the brain is far more powerful. It continually receives, records and stores information. Our brains are divided into two parts, the conscious and the subconscious. The conscious is the "awareness" part of our mind, always thinking, evaluating and wondering what's right or wrong, what's true or untrue.

The subconscious stores all our memories and experiences, good and bad. Our subconscious is programmed to accept all information and record it as fact. It doesn't question morality. The subconscious doesn't question. It accepts. So if information is repeated over and over, our subconscious doesn't ask whether it's true or untrue. It just stores the data as fact.

This is great if we only store positive emotions, but for most of us that's not reality. We have all stored negative thoughts in our subconscious since early childhood, including memories (real or perceived) and ideas that have been mulled over and over. If our parents and carers told us that we were stupid, if our teachers said that we were lazy or no good, these ideas were stored in our subconscious, in our belief system. This affects our pure radiant energy – our unsullied love for ourselves and others, our sense of self. We begin to doubt ourselves, question our reactions and fear the reactions of others. Little by little our lights dim and our energy learns to hide itself from others. Think of a moment when you know that happened to you as a child. Feel once more the pain of it – a humiliation, a wound from childhood. Feel yourself retreating. An unchallenged opinion, a subjective viewpoint can affect a whole life. The messages our brain receives become *fact*.

Let me tell you about positive thinking

We are programmed from childhood to believe certain things about ourselves. We have *learned* behaviours that condition us. We have grown the protective shell I spoke about earlier. Here's the good news: the Butterfly Experience can help you *unlearn* these behaviours. We don't have to keep believing those voices from the past. You can break out of your shell.

> Positive thinking means
> controlling your thought life,
> to achieve your personal destiny.

> Positive thinking means
> feeling in charge of your life, feeling full of joy.

> Positive thinking means
> creating a wish list and making it happen.

OK, hands up now. Perhaps there is a wee voice in the back of your head saying, "It's all right for her, but that psychobabble wouldn't work for me"? You're right – with that kind of attitude and negative thinking there is *no way* you can have an abundant life. You need to change your thinking. The Butterfly Experience frees the mind and prevents it from holding onto negative emotions, behaviours and attitudes.

Make a decision to START NOW. Choose to do the things you want. Have the career you want. Be in control of your life. Choose better health, higher energy levels, emotions that feel good. Coming through the Butterfly Experience you'll automatically develop a positive mindset. That mindset in turn will attract opportunities. And those changes will ripple out, affecting family, friends and colleagues.

I want to give you a powerful example of how what happens inside our hearts matters. After the terrible events of 9/11, people the world over sent America powerful, loving thoughts. I believe that this positive energy helped to heal America. Despite the suffering the people endured, the country was fizzing with a loving energy that eased the nation's pain. If a whole country can be helped to heal, what could you achieve in your life? Love (and what is positive thinking if not that?) is the strongest emotion that we have.

Love – that purest of energies – can heal the world. But it has to start with love of *self*. If we all loved ourselves and each other more, the energy throughout the entire world would change. There would be no more fighting, no more hunger, no more killing.

The healing can start with ourselves. The Butterfly Experience affects how you feel about yourself. It affects how you act, so your whole life improves. Just think of the joy a beautiful butterfly gives – and remember how short life is. Think change. Think butterfly!

CHAPTER THREE

Here's How the Butterfly Experience Works

YOU ARE BEGINNING to understand how you can use positive thinking to heal your body. You can *also* heal your spirit. In fact, when the spirit is balanced, the body follows. In choosing to explore the Butterfly Experience you've already begun to think positively. Here's the next step: by understanding how the subconscious influences thinking for good or bad, you can change your negative self-beliefs for the better. I want to help you to understand the mechanics of your mind. So now for the science bit ...

There are four different states of brain activity:

DELTA   BETA   ALPHA   THETA

You're probably thinking, "Sounds like a load of old Greek to me ...." But remember that you want to open up your mind to new concepts? Stay with me here ... These brain states are all happening within you, right now, whether you are aware of them or not. I want you to learn how to maximize them.

Delta is the slowest brain activity of the four states. The name makes me think of a river, slow moving, broadening out. This is the state of sleep and healing. When we're told to "sleep on it", this is the wisdom of the ages. Delta heals our bodies and our minds. In delta we are restored. Our mind is fully updated and reorganized. We awake the next morning refreshed and re-energized for what the day will bring.

Beta is the state of alertness and concentration, of being awake and logical. It allows you to think quickly, accessing information stored in the brain. We are in beta as we go about our everyday lives. At certain times beta heightens and the mind becomes more sharply focused – for example, when we're preparing to take exams, speak in public or compete in a sports contest. It is in this state that the physiological stress response, fight or flight, kicks in if we are faced with a difficult or dangerous situation. You are reading this book in beta. Thoughts and emotions are coming up in you all the time. For example, you may be frightened of self-relaxation, even though intellectually you understand its benefits. Change – or the status quo? Which are *you* going to choose?

Alpha governs visualization and relaxation. This is the state we need to be in to maximize the self-relaxation exercises I'm about to teach you. Brain activity slows down and even though we may *feel* half asleep, our awareness expands. This is the state of daydreaming that allows us to come up with new ideas and be creative. In alpha worries and fears disappear. Paradoxically, although we might seem at our most vulnerable in alpha, this is the strongest state of all. When our brain is in alpha it is at its most receptive, enabling us to access (usually without trying very hard) the "good stuff", the ideas that change our lives.

Theta governs meditation, memory and intuition. This is the state that follows relaxation. Brain activity slows down completely, though not to the point of sleep. This is the state where "the magic" happens. This is where we use our intuition, where we get new ideas and inspiration. In theta we access all those long-forgotten memories and mind pictures. We remember dreams, rediscover past events. In theta we can recall them easily, learn lessons from them. We learn to see the past with new eyes. Sometimes in theta we feel as if we are floating in our own inner world. This is the state in which we can reprogram our mind. In it we can access wonder and see ourselves living an astonishing life. Theta is the state of self-hypnosis. I can't overemphasize the importance of this state – it's the key to evolving, the key to positive thinking, the Holy Grail. It's the essence of spirituality, where we find ourselves and our Higher Self. Theta is where it all happens and we make positive changes that revolutionize our lives.

Excited? You should be!

De-clutter your thinking

Now that you have a clearer idea of how your mind works, let's use that information to help de-clutter your thinking. Don't let fear stop you. This stuff is uncomplicated

– if you want to feel happy, think happy thoughts. Mind-blowingly simple.

By now you're starting to really think about your own life. About what needs to change. That's good. But I know you need a little reassurance. Change – even the thought of it – can be very scary. I'm about to give you a precious gift that will help you to deal with any fears that arise as you move through the Butterfly Experience. I'm going to teach you how to *relax*.

> *Agenda for today: breathe out, breathe in and breathe out.*
>
> THE BUDDHA (*c.* 563–*c.* 483 BCE)

The philosopher and mathematician Blaise Pascal (1623–1662) believed that the world was an unhappy place because of people's "inability to sit quietly in a room". What if all you needed to be happy was to sit quietly?

We spend all our time and energy looking for power in externals, unaware of the power within ourselves. Just look at the way we discharge negative energy – through addictions, shopping, casual cruelty to others, harmful behaviours, unfulfilling sex. What if you didn't need designer labels or the latest technological gadget to be happy? What if you could find joy just by going inside yourself? What if you could connect with your purpose, knowing instinctively the part you need to play in the world?

Today you are going to learn to use a tool so vital to your well-being that you will wonder how you ever lived without it. My simple technique for self-relaxation will *change your life*. It is a gift that should be taught to every child in the world. It's called "going within". You're about to touch the pure energy within yourself. The real, unadulterated You.

The 6th-century BCE Chinese philosopher Lao Tzu said, "Muddy water, let stand, becomes clear." Our minds are cluttered with unimportant thoughts that rob us of pure energy. Only when our mind is still and empty can we fill it with happy, positive thoughts. The simple technique of self-relaxation that I teach you in this chapter harnesses that ability. It allows you to focus on what really matters.

Self-relaxation or meditation comes from Eastern philosophy, but people from all over the world can benefit from this simple technique. It requires discipline and perseverance, so establish it as part of your daily routine and follow through on it. Don't just give up after a few days. Embedding this spiritual discipline in your life will quickly pay dividends. You don't have to take my word for it. Buddhist monks, renowned for their calm and compassion, spend time going inward every day. So don't cheat yourself. Don't do what you've always done. Devote your energy to this; all change requires energy.

Even cloistered Buddhists have to contend with life's daily frustrations. Through meditation they learn control over their reactions. They learn to *choose* joy. They don't fear challenges. Instead, they look for the lessons to be learned. They *expect* to grow through their experiences. Through meditation the monks heal themselves, physically and mentally. They are probably the most disease-free people on the planet. Instead of fighting life, they go with its flow. This is self-relaxation at its best – a daily, conscious decision to focus on the positive.

One of the great teachings of Buddhism is recognizing that we cause much of our stress ourselves, through our expectations of ourselves and others. When we feel down, depressed or angry or simply that things are going wrong, we are usually out of touch with ourselves, our own energy, our own essence.

What if you could change your life by just being in the moment? What if that quiet time of self-relaxation made you a different person, with different values and a very different quality of life? It's time to take back control. It's time to avoid burnout, exhaustion and long-term illness. The next few pages will teach you how to relax and go inside yourself to discover the treasure within.

Self-relaxation is a perfectly natural state, just like day-dreaming. It's our richest source of ideas and inspiration. You don't need a guru or life coach or hypnotherapist to find it. You have the power to access it right now. Combine this technique with the visualization I'll teach you later (see pages 168–9) and you have a powerful force for good.

I can almost hear you saying, "Meditation? Tried that. Didn't work!" I can hear you groaning that you don't have enough time as it is. How much time do you spend glued to the TV or poring over celebrity magazines, wishing your life could be different?

Everyone, yes *everyone*, can find 15 minutes a day to radically improve their life. You have the choice right now. It's been said that the beginning of wisdom is the willingness to look at things in a different way. Throw off the negative thinking that's telling you, "This will never work", or "I feel foolish". Your Inner Child is ready. DO IT TODAY, otherwise tomorrow will just be a repeat of your current experience.

Everything starts with a conscious decision. Learning self-relaxation marks the beginning of a new chapter in your life. Commit to taking 10 to 15 minutes to practise each day, preferably in the morning. Be disciplined. Think of a deep-sea diver checking their air supply. Allow nothing to divert you from this quiet time. It will dictate the quality of your day.

The only thought you need to have right now is "change". Understand that what you have been doing up till now hasn't been enough for you. You need new thinking, new ideas, new practices. Forget everything you think you know about self-relaxation and meditation. Accept that there is no right or wrong way to do things. The way you choose to proceed is the right way for you. I've seen people spend large amounts of money and untold hours in stress management courses, coming away more frustrated than ever. This is different.

This is the start of a new, positive routine. Again, I want to emphasize that you will feel the difference immediately. You will become calm, relaxed and more focused in your thought processes.

Self-relaxation and self-hypnosis are the same thing. Both terms describe a light trance, an altered state of the mind. The purpose of self-relaxation is to make our minds calm and peaceful. It is the most important thing that we can do to help ourselves. Self-relaxation will actually slow your heart rate. It will make your thinking more focused and alert. It will energize you. Instead of waiting for happy times we can *create* them using this technique. Everyone can do it – in fact we all do it automatically. I'm asking you to lay aside all prejudices. If for any reason you have to awaken during the relaxation, you can do so by simply opening your eyes. You will be fully awake. You can return to your self-relaxation at a later time.

For now, just go with the instructions on the next few pages. They will *change* your life.

Read through this exercise and then you are ready to practise. Be prepared to amaze yourself.

Self-relaxation

Find a quiet place to sit and make yourself comfortable. Choose a chair that allows you to sit with a straight back in order to align your spine and let your feet rest on the floor. Remove your glasses if you wear them. You will soon come to feel your own energy and feel very at peace. This feeling will grow each time you do your self-relaxation. Before you begin, decide on three affirmations (positive statements in the present tense), such as:

I am a confident person.

I approve of myself.

I am healthy and happy.

1. Allow yourself to relax. Feel your body supported by the chair. In your own time allow your eyes to close comfortably.

2. Become aware of your breathing. Breathe in, and on every out-breath slowly and mentally start counting from "ten". Breathe in and on the out-breath mentally count "nine", all the way down to "one". You will become more relaxed – 10 percent more relaxed with each descending number.

3. Staying deeply relaxed you will soon find that your mind begins to wander, maybe to a favourite place. Your mind will choose the right place for you – no need to fight the thought. It may be a beach, a garden or a favourite room. You aren't bound to it – from time to time the place you use, your inner sanctuary, may change. Your mind will automatically wander to the safest place, where you feel most secure.

4. Imagine a white light shining down from above and allow it to melt down through your head, through the seventh chakra, which is referred to as the crown. It is located on top of the skull. According to Eastern traditions, this chakra is the energy centre of your spirituality and is associated with the colour purple or white. We use this chakra as a tool to communicate with our spiritual nature, and it is sometimes referred to as our God Source. Let the white light melt down to the tip of your toes, bringing you calm, peace and contentment. Spend time there. Relax. Unwind. Feel the white light re-energize your body; allow your body to refocus.

5. You may experience a floating sensation. Don't worry. It's simply a sign that your body is relaxing. You may experi-

ence a sensation of warmth, perceive smells or even see colours. Spend time in this state, giving yourself positive affirmations, making positive statements about yourself to yourself.

6. Choose one thing in your life to focus on and make sure it's realistic. Now, imagine yourself the way you want to be. If you have a problem, see it fixed. See yourself living the life you want. See yourself content, smiling, healthier. See the job, the house, the holidays, the family you want – feel as if you are already this person living that life. Allow the pure energy of that feeling to enter every muscle and cell in your body. You can go to this place at any time, on any day you choose. This is your space, your special place.

7. To awaken yourself, count from one to ten. At the count of eight, open your eyes. Tell yourself that you feel refreshed, re-energized, and more confident. You feel more in control. You have a greater sense of well-being.

FEEL HOW GOOD THAT WAS!

Feel the difference

Claim those precious 10 to 15 minutes every day and watch your life change. This Butterfly Experience technique changes you at a fundamental, cellular level. It will change you at a psychological level – as soon as you begin to use self-relaxation to improve your mindset, you'll wonder why you never did it before. You'll find space in your head to look at where you are going and even begin to see possibilities of how to get there. Most importantly, it will change you at a spiritual level.

Self-relaxation is the most therapeutic tool you can learn. It calms your mind, which controls your emotions. Our thoughts give birth to our feelings. We're not responsible for the thoughts we have. But we *are* responsible for how long we hold onto them. When we learn to train our minds, it becomes easy to replace our negative thoughts with positive ones. We become more balanced. Acquiring this skill can bring new emotions to the surface. Don't be afraid of them. The word "emotion" comes from the Latin *emovere*, meaning "to move". Emotions are meant to serve us, not the other way around. They are there to help us to move through life, to help us to understand ourselves and our needs. So no more hiding from the truth of your emotions – begin to look to them as a source of wisdom.

Success with this technique breeds success in life. People who use it gain acceptance of themselves. They see clearly what they need to do to move on. They make positive changes and transform their lives for the better. They choose to be happy and relaxed, fulfilled. They choose to deal with problems instead of allowing themselves to become over-whelmed by them.

Start living your new life today. It only takes a little courage and a little faith.

CHAPTER FOUR

Butterfly Experience Affirmations

I HAVE ALREADY SPOKEN about the subconscious and its role in our happiness. By using Butterfly Experience Affirmations, you can train your mind to be more positive. These are simple, positive statements that we repeat to ourselves over and over until we start to believe them.

Butterfly Experience Affirmations will change your whole belief system. Change your habitual thinking for the better, and you change your life for the better. The brain is made up of tiny nerve cells called neurons, which connect to create neural pathways. These connections form our ideas, thoughts and memories. The more you use a function, the stronger the neural pathway becomes. In other words, your behaviours are formed through repetition – and these can be created using the Butterfly Experience Affirmations. That is why it is so important to give yourself positive statements about yourself. If you believe that you don't deserve to live in a beautiful home, the chances are that you don't like where you're currently living. It's no one's fault that you have this belief. But it's your responsibility to do something about it.

It's vital that we start off the day in the right way, by programming our subconscious. Whenever I begin work with my clients I ask them to use positive affirmations. These are very powerful, positive statements said in the present tense. They are especially wonderful when we're low and need a pick-me-up. I tell clients to repeat their affirmation to themselves three times on awakening. For example:

I am feeling confident.

I am feeling happy.

I am calm and full of pure energy.

The Butterfly Experience asks us to choose three positive affirmations to say each day. I know for some of you this may feel strange – outlandish even. But look at it this way – what you've been doing up till now hasn't been working properly, otherwise you wouldn't be reading this book. Each of us is searching for that elusive "something", the missing piece of the jigsaw that, when it clicks into place, will make all our wishes come true. That "something" lies deep inside you right now. You can be happy, healthy, confident, positive and abundantly rich, starting right now – just trust the process.

It is important for you to write down your Butterfly Experience Affirmations as this reinforces the message in your mind. Remember that you are working only on *your* self-belief system and vibrational energy. Others need to do this work for themselves. When you are meditating you can ask in general terms for help for others, but focus on your own needs and desires.

By using Butterfly Experience Affirmations you will start to change the habitual patterns of your mind. Affirmations change the negative beliefs that you hold deep within your subconscious. Our mindset is paramount. Here are a few of my own favourite Butterfly Experience Affirmations to inspire you:

I am open and willing to change.

I love myself exactly as I am.

I am filled with abundance.

Pure energy is flowing through my body.

Say your Butterfly Experience Affirmations with feeling and emotion. Really mean them. As you say them you may not be feeling happy. Remember that we can "trick" the sub-conscious – if you say something, your subconscious will believe it. Before you know it, you will be behaving like a happy person. Your attitude will have changed. You will act and feel as if you are that person you've visualized, confident and healthy.

Several written exercises now follow to help you.

JOURNAL: EXERCISE ONE

Your Butterfly Experience Affirmations

Choose up to three areas in your life that you would most like to enhance. For example, money, career and weight.

- Turn to your Butterfly Experience Journal at the back of the book and write down one Butterfly Experience Affirmation for each area. For example: "Money flows easily and freely to me." Repeat them three times each, both morning and night, every day for 21 days. Say them with feeling. Believe them.

- Write down in your Butterfly Experience Journal how you would feel if each affirmation was already manifest in your life. For example: "I have a wonderful new job and am filled with happiness." You may still be looking for the perfect job, but by saying your Butterfly Experience Affirmation you'll have more energy to find it.

HAVE YOU SAID YOUR
BUTTERFLY EXPERIENCE AFFIRMATIONS
FOR TODAY?

Examine your life

Now that you've learned to relax and lift your mood, you'll be feeling in a more positive frame of mind. It's time to really focus on your life. For your Butterfly Experience Blueprint you need to establish where you are, right this moment.

Remember, it doesn't matter what anyone else thinks. We're looking for the steps *you* need to take to be happier. So let's get started.

JOURNAL: EXERCISE TWO

What Makes You Happy?

Everyone wants to be happy, but how many of us have actually asked ourselves, "What does happiness mean to me?" or, "What specifically would bring me happiness?" Take a few minutes to think about it. Don't rush this exercise – it's a spiritual building block.

- Turn to your Butterfly Experience Journal and write down three things that make your happy. For example, meeting a friend for lunch, going on holiday or watching a good movie. Think about the little things in life that make you happy. Remember when you were a child, playing on a swing, feeling the air rush by you? That feeling of freedom was *enough*. No cares or worries ... What does that for you today?

- Now write down three actions you need to take to make you happy. For example, phone a friend to arrange a lunch date, make arrangements for a long-earned holiday or simply make time to watch your favourite movie.

JOURNAL: EXERCISE THREE

What Would Improve Your Life?

Now take a moment to think of what you want to *change* to improve your life. The Butterfly Experience asks you to think now about every area of your life – job satisfaction, relationships, leisure time, ambitions ... Ask yourself to be really honest. Where do you feel you're in a rut? Are you happy at work? Do you enjoy the friends you have? What about your relationships – are they working? Do they sustain you? Face up to the truth of your life. Be ruthlessly honest. Do you have weight issues? Debts? A mother-in-law who makes you feel vulnerable?

- Seven is a magical number, so turn to your Butterfly Experience Journal and write down seven things in your life that need changing. Remember that the butterfly undergoes a repeated process of several metamorphoses and discarding before it can take flight. So show your commitment to change by writing them down – especially those things you've never really admitted to anyone else. Give each of the seven areas of your life a mark out of ten. Don't be frightened – this list is just for you. You are in control. All we need is seven honest admissions.

- Notice how your body reacts, especially if you say them out loud. Feel how your body tightens in fear or frustration or anger. This is your body's gift, telling you not to accept these things any more. Your body is telling you to make some serious decisions.

- Change begins with a single thought. You've just agreed certain aspects of your life are making you miserable. Step out your comfort zone – that's where growth starts. It's not as scary as you think. You may even like it. By writing down your honest thoughts about your life, you take power away from the negative and give it to the positive. You know what's not working and what needs to change. You have greater self-awareness.

- Now that you have admitted you want to change, let's get started doing just that. HOW? By becoming open to new ideas.

- Let's go back to your list. Identify what things in your life make you feel really negative and decide to get rid of them *today*. Identify and weed out the friends who are pulling you down. Decide to detach from any negative energy. Decide to stop doing the things that make you unhappy. If you're being taken advantage of, decide to find a way of sharing the load with others. This is your life – it's too precious to waste. From the seven areas that you have identified, choose the one that you most need to change and write it down. Write down three actions that you can take to improve that area.

JOURNAL: EXERCISE FOUR

Count Your Blessings

Now I want you to think of all the good things you have in your life. It's an old-fashioned idea I'm hoping to teach the world again. It's called counting your blessings. We're all too caught up in the material world. We think that if we have a bigger house and a faster car, or if we win the lottery, we'll be happy. Well, I have news for you. Happiness cannot be bought – but you can get it for free. What do you have to be grateful for? Right here, right now? Health, a home, a loving family, a career, food on the table ...? These are the things that should make you happy.

- Write down the things that your life has been blessed with – create a gratitude list.

- Now write down three things you're good at. This is no time for false modesty. You're building your future happiness here. What are your gifts? What comes easily to you? What do you enjoy? We often don't give these things a second thought, but they are blessings too. Rejoice in them.

- Now that you know how to count your blessings, you've made a start in thinking about yourself and your life in a more positive manner. Now that you know you have so many things to be grateful for, start acting that way. Show Spirit that you're grateful for these blessings, many of which you may have been taking for granted. You're growing and learning. See what the universe has given you already? Why would it not give you more?

JOURNAL: EXERCISE FIVE

What Do You Really Want in Life?

Change is already happening. Gifts have begun "flying at your through the darkness". The caterpillar is starting to gnaw its way out of the shell. Time for another list.

It's time to start thinking about what you really want from life. Think about the butterfly, its beautiful, vibrant colours, its effortless joy-giving quality. What would make you take flight?

- In your Butterfly Experience Journal, start writing your wish list under the words "I desire". A list, by definition, includes more than one item. This is no time to be shy. This is your life; believe that the universe will provide all that you want. Remember, it's all waiting inside you. Look into your heart. Search out your truest, innermost desires. Need some inspiration? What makes you feel excited when you think about it? What dreams did you have as a child that you've since let go? Where would you go and what would you do tomorrow if money were no object? Add the dreams you'd be too embarrassed to admit even to your best friend – the more outlandish the better. Think really hard. What do you really want? No matter how far off these desires seem today, get them down on paper. Something magical happens when we write things down. They acquire power. Soon you're going to start to make these dreams grow. I'm going to show you how to nurture them. You'll see that they're not so remote after all.

- Now write down three actions you need to take to achieve your desires.

- Now write down the things you wanted to do and have in your life and regret not doing.

- Write down three actions you need to take to start achieving them.

- In your Butterfly Experience Journal, date and sign your statement affirming that you are willing to be open to change.

Look at what you've done already. Five Butterfly Experience exercises and now you have some vital information – information that people go a lifetime without:

- You know what you have to be grateful for.

- You know what's working for you and what's not.

- You know *what you want*.

Congratulations on completing the first five exercises of your Butterfly Experience Journal. Now it's time to take the next step and start creating and accepting the rewards that life has in store for you.

JOURNAL: EXERCISE SIX

Create the Life You Deserve

This exercise is an "inside job". If you are to create the life you deserve, you need a starting place. Your character and your unique set of abilities are that place. Give this exercise energy. It will balance your sense of self and help you to recognize positive aspects that you've long forgotten. It will also show you the aspects that need attention. This is a precious tool. Take it seriously.

- Give me a list of the best qualities you possess and all the things you are good at. It's time to take stock of what you have and what you'll need.

- Now look over the list. Thank yourself for your best qualities. Each gift is needed if we are to achieve our full potential and help others to grow. Claim them as yours.

- Write down the three actions you need to take to improve your life.

JOURNAL: EXERCISE SEVEN

What's Good About You?

When a butterfly lays its eggs they're held firmly in place by a special, glue-like substance that keeps the new life safe and allows it to grow. So what's the glue that will hold your new life together? I'm talking about self-belief, confidence.

Confidence isn't as elusive as you think. *To be a confident person all we have to do is accept ourselves for who we are.* Each of us is a one-off, a combination of unique gifts and talents. People who are confident believe in their own abilities. Self-belief attracts more opportunities. Being open to what life has to offer makes us feel stronger, so that we become more confident. The key is believing that you are worthy.

- I want you to sieve your way through your own thoughts about yourself. Write down seven positive thoughts. As you're writing, I want you to pick out straightaway any negatives that arise. Now that you recognize the negative thoughts about yourself, it'll be possible to recognize them again if they appear in the future. Put them to the side for the moment. Finish your list of seven positive qualities.

- Start to see the real you emerging. These exercises are vital, because they uncover your truth. They reveal your Spirit. You can see what you have to offer the world on paper, in black and white. Recognize and claim these things. Your natural character, abilities and desires are your precious gifts. The Butterfly Experience is going to help you develop them, develop you, develop your dreams. If you stay true to your natural character, you can achieve anything. No matter what happens, or who tries to put you down, if you believe in yourself, stay true to yourself, your life will change.

JOURNAL: EXERCISE EIGHT

Back to Basics

Turn again to your Butterfly Experience Journal and the seven categories of your life that you examined in Exercise Three – for example, career, family, relationships and finance. It's time to focus on these areas.

- Write down Butterfly Experience Affirmations for each category. For example:

Career
**I am a hard worker
properly rewarded for my efforts.**

Home
I am happily married with a wonderful family.

Social life
I have caring friends.

Finance
I am able to pay my bills easily.

Spirituality
I am aligned with Spirit.

Now that you've written these affirmations, I want you to *use* them. Remember that these are your personal mantras.

Seven spiritual tasks

We're coming to the end of this first stage on your journey. Here are seven spiritual tasks that I want you to begin building into your day.

Task One: Refer to your good points

From now on, refer daily to your list of good points. Add to it as new thoughts occur to you. Write down compliments you receive and good things that people have said about you. Each day look at the list of things you want to get rid of or improve. You may want to boost your self-image or lose some weight. Perhaps you want to create better relationships. Your awareness of these areas has been raised, so start working on them. Look for opportunities to bring positive experiences into your life and remember to use your self-relaxation (see pages 30–32) and Butterfly Experience Affirmations (see page 34–7) to help you.

Task Two: Act confidently

"Fake it until you make it". If you act confidently, people respond to you differently. We teach others how to treat us by means of our attitude and our body language. The following stage will teach you more about these vital skills. For now practise standing tall each day, look people in the eye and smile! Remember that others may be feeling as nervous as you are. You don't need a title to be important. All you need to be happy is already within you.

Task Three: Mix with positive people

Surround yourself with positive, confident people. Seek them out. Model aspects of them. Your own confidence will grow as a result. My mother is always positive. Through her I learned the value of positive thinking. I admire her so much for her strength of character. The positive lessons she taught me as a child have stayed with me all my life. My whole childhood rang with phrases such as: "Keep going, even when times are hard", "Never give up!" and "Your reward is waiting just over the hill."

Task Four: Accept yourself

Accept who you are today – and remember that this is just the beginning. We are all under constant pressure to be the perfect shape, to be glamorous, rich and successful, to have perfect teeth and wonderful families. Yet if we look around, how many of us approach that ideal? Instead of feeling shy, weak or insecure, see yourself as a valuable human being. Acknowledge the fact that you've been doing your best and that you're changing. Your attitude toward yourself will change very quickly.

Task Five: Seek out opportunity

Grab opportunities with both hands. Everyday life gives us chances – but we're often too afraid to capitalize on them. Each day go to different places, look to make new friends. Jumping over our own shyness and inhibitions is vital –

break through that shell! You don't have to perform. Just ask others questions about themselves. Show an interest in them, instead of worrying about the impression you're making. A small change in perspective, but it can bring huge dividends.

Task Six: Live for today

Stop taking your life for granted. LIVE EVERY DAY AS IF IT WERE YOUR LAST! Ask yourself, "What could I do today that would make me feel happy and proud?" Take a step toward it. To be esteemed you have to act in an estimable way. Nothing gives us a healthier sense of self than helping others. Think of something you could do to make a difference in someone else's life. And don't take credit for it!

Task Seven: Choose the positive

Every day of your life gives you additional knowledge that takes you further on your journey. What have you learned to date? Is there a negative that's holding you back today? Do you hold grudges toward family, friends or colleagues? Are you bitter about some unresolved conflict? Feel the weight that you're carrying. Remember that it doesn't have to be that way. All it takes is the realization that you're hurting yourself time and time again by reliving the initial hurt. Let it go now. It's time.

The realizations and choices made at this foundation stage in the Butterfly Experience journey provide you with everything you need to move beyond your protective shell and on to the next stage of growth. But before you finish this stage, I want to talk now about a vital element of your life that you may have been overlooking in your search for growth. Again, it's in the last place you might have thought to look – inside yourself. It's one of our most precious gifts and it's called intuition.

CHAPTER FIVE

Trusting Your Intuition

THE BUTTERFLY EXPERIENCE demands that we relearn this skill. Every human being has this sixth sense – we talk about a "gut feeling", an inner reaction that tells us what's right. Our gift of intuition or inner wisdom is so precious, yet as adults we frequently ignore it. Children, on the other hand, use their intuition all the time; they are so open and intuitive. But as they grow older they are pressurized to act in different ways and begin to turn from it. Advances in science and technology have benefited society greatly, but intangibles like intuition have been neglected. We've forgotten how to trust this great gift.

Our ability to connect with our Higher Self has been lost. It's our built-in safety mechanism, the voice of Spirit who wants the very best for us. But here's the good news. Once we reconnect with it, the more we use our intuition, the more it develops. Sonia Choquette, author of *Trust Your Vibes*, talks of human beings in terms of five- and six-sensory people. I call myself a six-sensory person, because I've listened to my intuition all my life, knowing that if something doesn't feel right I should walk away.

Have you ever intuitively feared something but dismissed that fear? And then paid the price? That feeling you ignored was your body's ancient wisdom. We sometimes use phrases like, "I had a weird feeling" or "I had this odd sensation". Why not just come out and say it was your intuition? There are dozens of expressions – from "Sleep on it" to "If in doubt, leave it out" – that bear this idea out.

Can you imagine the consequences of relying more deeply on this inner knowing? Can you imagine using it in your daily life? For example, listening to people and intuitively knowing the right thing to do or say; hearing about a set of circumstances and intuitively knowing whether you want to be part of it or not; knowing what would bring you joy or sadness. Our intuition is also known as our "third eye", a centre of knowingness that some people believe is located between the eyebrows.

When you connect with your intuition, it is as though your life has been switched on. No one can teach you this skill – you have to feel it for yourself. You'll know when you find it.

To tap back into that intuition, I want you to learn and build on all the Butterfly Experience techniques I'm teaching you. Practise them daily. With just a little persistence you will see changes almost immediately. You can't understand how powerful these techniques are unless you try them. You need to reject negative thinking at a cellular level. You need to be ruthless, accepting only the best of yourself.

To do that, you must learn to be discerning. You need to understand what strengthens and what weakens you. So if you've just been reading these pages and not *doing* the work, go back now and do it. Think about what's on offer here. A few hours to change your entire life? How can you *not* do it? Aren't you worth it?

Give yourself permission to become whole. Wipe the slate clean and start again. You only have to become willing to change and then the universe will help you. You don't need to worry about how or when. It will happen in universal time. If you start today then you are one day closer to that dream.

Only move on to the Caterpillar stage when you've completed the work in the Egg stage – when you understand who you are and what you want, and have admitted what has stopped you achieving your goals so far.

When you've completed the work in this first stage, I want you to cement your commitment to the process by signing the written contract overleaf. This is not a half-hearted, I-kind-of-get-what-she's-talking-about pie-crust promise that is easily made and broken. I'm talking about a firm contract with yourself, to act and think more positively in life. In *all* areas of your life. It's time to draw that line in the sand. *Make the choice today* to make the most of the Butterfly Experience and change your life.

MAKE A COMMITMENT
TO YOURSELF HERE AND NOW!

Contract

I agree today to be willing to be open to change.

Each day I attract new opportunities and abundance.

Signature: ....

Date: ....

STAGE TWO · THE CATERPILLAR

Growing Pains

———————

CHAPTER SIX

Growth

By now you've grown in your awareness of your strengths – you know that you're able to survive outside the protective walls you have created. Although the thought of change seems scary, remember the alternative. You can stay a caterpillar for ever. Never be a butterfly. It's your choice.

If we resist "change", we're flowing against universal energy. Things change all the time, and often change brings things that we welcome. Think about all the positive changes that you've already experienced in life – your first love perhaps, or the time you developed a new skill or discovered an unexpected talent. Remember that new job, new car, new friend, new experience? Change within the Butterfly Experience means making choices, taking action and stepping out to create opportunities that will bring you happiness.

The Caterpillar stage helps you to look at your life and decide what to keep and what to jettison. What I'm offering you in this section is personal freedom – no more, no less. It's time to expand and grow. It's time to shed the negative. Caterpillars grow at a phenomenal rate, so you should expect rapid growth in this part of the cycle, too.

Just as butterflies are different from species to species, caterpillars also differ. Some are downright dull, easily overlooked. Some manage to camouflage themselves better than others. Some are experts at hiding. Some caterpillars go quietly about their business. Others have bright stripes that warn predators to keep away. Some have bristles or spikes, and seem downright menacing. Which kind of caterpillar are you? What are you hiding behind? What do you need to shed in order to grow? It's time to talk about …

Owning our emotions

We all experience painful events. Without knowing life's darker side, we cannot fully know its joys. It's a common reaction for people to shrug off past hurts. Some of our hurts become so deeply buried we manage to convince ourselves that we're over them. But unless you deal with those hurts, those repressed, confused emotions are all you're giving your subconscious to work with. The Butterfly Experience asks you to consider how you react to the past *today*. If thinking about past hurts is still hurting you, you need to find a way to move on.

In the Butterfly Experience we learn to think of thoughts and emotions as the building blocks for your new life. Caterpillars are like machines – they nourish themselves and simultaneously get rid of whatever they don't need. So this section is about finding out what's stored in your subconscious that is causing you pain. What thinking do you need to jettison? This is where the Butterfly Experience starts to get tough. The human ego wants us to avoid pain at all cost. It doesn't want us to go to that painful place, so we rationalize, justify, excuse, blame and do whatever it takes to stop ourselves feeling the very painful emotions that will eventually heal us. And so the bad feelings stay inside and eat away at us. In the Caterpillar stage you will identify and work your way through these painful feelings.

Just as what we eat today shapes our body in the future, so what we think today dictates our emotional security – our happiness for tomorrow. Deprived of spiritual nourishment, our minds struggle. Most of us spend more time on our cars than on our mental processes. We buy senseless stuff for our homes. We waste money on clothes in order to impress others. We burden ourselves with debt, all for the sake of what other people think. The Caterpillar stage will allow you to look at these things and evaluate them for what they are. Above all, this stage will teach you to watch your thoughts. We are so conscious nowadays of what we need to eat to stay healthy. What we need to realize is that it's just as important to feed our minds. Louise L. Hay, well known as one of the founders of the self-help movement, says our thoughts create our lives.

The Butterfly Experience asks you to be much more conscious of your thought processes. How and what you think determines your future. The quality of your life depends on it. If you don't check your thinking for faults, this new life you're constructing won't be sound. It is so important to feed your mind positive language. Think about your self-talk. How often do you tell yourself, "I feel awful and I really don't look good"? What do you think your subconscious mind does with that negative information? It acts accordingly.

Grudging acceptance of this idea won't bring about the changes you need in your life. Remember how strongly the subconscious holds on to ideas. Here's a powerful example.

After a night of heavy drinking out on the town, a young man had become embroiled in an incident, in which another man was stabbed. The young man had suffered a blackout and was being held responsible. Desperate, he approached a clinical hypnotherapist.

Could the hypnotherapist help him recall the events of the evening? After his session, the young man was fully able to remember the incident *and* his role in it. That's the power of the subconscious. *It holds on to those things that the conscious brain forgets.*

It's here that the Butterfly Experience comes into its own. It positively influences this part of our psyche. We learn to accept and let go of negative feelings, the things that threaten our happiness and our equilibrium. It helps us to find and enjoy balance in life. Over the years I have seen so much ill-health that could have been avoided if people had only understood the damage they were doing by holding on to anger and ill feeling. Store up enough rancour over a lifetime and you are guaranteed disease.

Caterpillar asks us to choose the positive, to choose joy, to choose growth. As the caterpillar hatches it begins to eat, nourishing itself with good things. From now on, I want you to choose only what nourishes you. As the caterpillar devours all the bounty Nature offers, it grows. Gradually its exoskeleton becomes too tight for comfort, so it sheds its skin, revealing new growth underneath. The stage between each of these sheddings goes by a wonderful name – "instar". The word makes me think of all the potential within us.

After each instar, each transformation, the caterpillar is different. It may change dramatically, in colour and appearance, from the instar before.

CHAPTER SEVEN

Negative Thoughts Grow with Attention

WHEN WE ALLOW SMALL negative thoughts to grow they soon become mighty negative thoughts. Our mood swings, and everything seems to fall apart. Be honest. What pain has had you reaching for the biscuit tin recently? What did your spouse say that made you shout at the children? What were you thinking just before you cut in front of that car on the road? Our days are full of thoughts that trigger negative behaviour.

Henry Ford (1863–1947) said that a clean engine always delivers power. As soon as you realize that you are responsible for your own happiness and unhappiness, you can begin to take control of your thoughts and your attitude. This section will ask you to become a "thought detective", to watch your every thought.

You need to be ruthless about these building blocks of thought. You need to face up to some unpleasant truths, acknowledge wrong behaviours and release yourself and others from situations you're trapped in emotionally. Anger and bitterness chain us. In order to be free, there are spiritual rules that have to be observed. These rules apply to all situations and at all times. There are no exceptions. Ask yourself, "How free do I want to be?"

The Caterpillar stage in this book offers spiritual and practical advice that is vital to your happiness, your health and your relationships. "Vital" means "necessary to life" – the new life that you want. Again, a reminder, this is the Butterfly Experience: you committed to change. If *you* don't change, *nothing* changes. Let this time be different. Let this be the time your Spirit gets what it needs. Let's start by looking at how you can ...

Learn to forgive yourself

We all make mistakes. "To err is human" is an ancient spiritual axiom. But too many of us seem unable to forgive ourselves. Think right now of someone you know who can't let go of the past. See how remorse and bitterness have marked them. Perhaps those negative emotions have metamorphosed into a depression. I see this so often in my clients, but it doesn't have to be that way for you. Admitting we were wrong requires a little humility. We can only move forward if we look honestly at our past and acknowledge the role we played in any difficulties.

Learn to forgive others

After an argument or disagreement, even if things are "reconciled", a residue of anger can remain. Controlling our thinking also means honouring our emotions. We have a right to our feelings. Peacemakers don't pretend that bad situations haven't happened. They admit where they were at fault and approach others in that spirit. Honest communication and a "win–win" attitude to solving problems will take you a long way.

If we could learn to forgive without waiting for the other person to come to us first, the world would be changed overnight. If we take the first step, the other person almost always takes the second. You know the saying "Life's too short"? Well, it will be even shorter if you hold on to grudges. They are the main culprits in negative thinking. And they destroy our health, literally making us live shorter lives. Is it worth dying because you can't forgive? Is there a situation in your life that an attitude of forgiveness could resolve? Who do you need to forgive so that you can free your energy and change your behaviour patterns? Or do you think that you don't need to forgive?

Make today the beginning of a new thought pattern – say your Butterfly Experience Affirmations and free yourself. For example:

I am open to forgiveness.

I am now free of resentments.

Write down the name of the person whom you need to forgive. Really think about the statement you are making. Start to feel the freedom this brings.

Learn to say sorry quickly

In my experience, people who struggle with forgiveness find it very hard to forgive themselves. They regard saying sorry as failure. In fact it is the kindest thing they can do – for themselves and others. Don't allow situations to worsen by waiting for the other person to make the first move. None of us knows what's really going on in someone else's life. Look to learn from every situation – has the person you're angry with got a point? Is there something you could learn from looking at the problem a different way? Be open to others' points of view. "Sorry" is such a small word, but it changes lives.

Learn your own lessons

Perhaps you've learned negative behaviour and habits from parents or friends. You've watched them hold on to anxieties. Or you're full of anger on their behalf. Remember, this is their lesson. If you diminish it in any way, if you enable them to get through a situation, they will just have to learn the lesson again. If you're over-involved in anyone else's life lesson, back out gracefully and use your energy to improve your own situation instead.

Learn to let go

Holding on to the past long term can destroy your happiness. Ironically, while we're holding on to anger, the people we are angry at are carrying on with their own lives. It's too easy to blame others for our problems. Is there a situation in your life that you refuse to let go? Is the emotional energy that you keep feeding making you miserable? Maybe you'll never get the apology that you want, maybe the truth will never be recognized. But so long as you allow the situation to control your thinking you will never be fully happy. Trust life to resolve the situation – trust the karmic process that what we give is returned to us sevenfold. It's time to use all that energy in a positive way. Learn to let go. All it takes is a decision. Repeat your Butterfly Experience Affirmations. For example:

I release all need to know the answers.

**I am comfortable not yet knowing
why this has happened.**

**I trust Spirit in this situation
to bring me peace.**

Think about a situation that you have carried around too long. The first one that comes to mind, go with it. Start with whatever comes up, then work through any other situations you have been holding on to where you need to learn to forgive and let go. The truth is that once you let go of the situation then your energy changes and you are more free to live your life abundantly and healthily.

Learn to stand up for what you need

Decide your own priorities. For a long time I had wanted to end my marriage. I didn't leave for fear of hurting my parents. For seven years I stayed, trying ways to make it work, becoming more and more miserable. Finally I made the decision to end it, but I dreaded telling my parents. I'll never forget my mother's words: "Sit down and I'll get us a cup of tea." If I had known she would be so accepting, I would have left years before. Instead, I wasted years *thinking*, allowing my thoughts to run away with themselves and become my truth. My truth was wrong.

Begin to stand up for what you need in little things – show integrity. Build on this idea gradually, promising yourself that you'll never again ignore the small voice inside that says, "This isn't right." If something is wrong or something is hurting you, say so.

Learn to let others be themselves

You can't change people – or the past. But you can change your attitude. Are you willing to sell your peace of mind for the sake of feeling vindicated? You *know* you're right, so let it go! Are you holding on to any negative experiences? Sometimes we nurture ill-feeling, because it makes us feel vindicated. It allows us to continue seeing others in a negative way, so we don't have to look at our own behaviour. Had a row with a friend? Instead of walking away, ask yourself why they acted the way they did. When we're hurting, we lash out. Why not let go of the hurt and let the healing start with you? A little hug could be all it takes to turn the situation around.

It is important to realize that it is *you* who suffers when you hold onto negative experiences, not the other person.

The energy is trapped within *you*. Now is the moment to take that step toward freedom. Rejoice. You deserve the best in life. Only by learning to be the best person you can, will you live a rich life. So drop your expectations of others. Release them and release yourself. There is so much better to come. Spirit has plans that you could never even dream of, so free yourself to be able to follow them.

So many people get into the mindset that everything always has to be "perfect". What *is* perfect? From where I'm standing, everything in life always turns out exactly the way it should – no matter whether the outcome is thought to be good or bad at the time. Everything in the universe is interconnected. It's not a case of bad things happening to good people. The universe gives us opportunities to learn and grow. Change what you can, *if* you can. If you can't change it, why get upset about it? There's a wonderful saying: "God, grant me the serenity to accept the things I cannot change, courage to accept the things I can, and the wisdom to know the difference."

Learn from experience

Find someone you can share negative experiences with – someone you can trust. It is so important to share our real emotions with another human being. Value your feelings enough to share them with another person and to benefit from their insight and wisdom. If you had the solution, you'd have used it by now.

The only way of putting negative experiences behind us

is to learn from them. No one escapes pain of one kind or another. Whatever the pain, time is the healer. But we can help process an experience by learning from it. Buddhists believe that our real purpose for being here is to learn the lessons that we still need to learn. They know that acceptance is the key. Everything that happens is designed to teach us. There is no failure if we learn from every experience, ensuring that we never repeat our mistakes. At this vital part of the Caterpillar stage, it's crucial that we develop the habit of using these experiences, searching for the pearl of wisdom to be gained. But ultimately we have to let the pain go.

Finish each day and be done with it. You have done what you could. Some blunders and absurdities no doubt crept in; forget them as soon as you can. Tomorrow is a new day; begin it well and serenely and with too high a spirit to be encumbered with your old nonsense.

RALPH WALDO EMERSON (1803–1882)

Learn to be fully in the present

It's a universal law that any negative energy we send out comes straight back. It's the boomerang effect. Like attracts like. To break free from unhappiness, you have to bring yourself fully into the present. You must accept that the past is just that – it's past. Deciding to let go is the hard part. Once that decision is made, life becomes easier.

MAKE A CONSCIOUS DECISION TODAY,

NO MATTER WHAT'S GOING ON IN YOUR LIFE,

TO LEAVE THE PAST BEHIND AND MOVE ON.

THANK THE UNIVERSE FOR

THE LESSONS YOU HAVE LEARNED.

Stay positive

Now that you've completed the spiritual exercises above, you need to learn to maintain positive thinking and positive energy through awareness. We need daily awareness of where we are emotionally and spiritually. Travelling through life going just one degree off course every day would mean we never arrive at our true destination.

Be the change you want to see in the world.
MAHATMA GANDHI (1869–1948)

Butterflies cannot be burdened if they are to fly. Facing up to our own negative thinking isn't easy because with it comes the realization that we've been causing ourselves harm. But the good news is that negativity can stop as of now. To become a happier person, you must first *believe*

that happiness is possible. That belief comes from understanding that you're as happy on any given day as you make
up your mind to be. Look at children – sad one minute and
the next their tears have dried and they're getting on with
the business of living. We all need to learn to let go the way
that children do.

Remember, the more attention we give to negative emotions, the worse we are going to feel. The more negative
the thought, the bigger it seems. We sink into a morass of
self-doubt and self-pity. And the vicious cycle starts all over
again. If you're thinking (and this is the last resort of the
ego), "It's too late for me", know this: you're never too old to
let go of emotional baggage.

I deserve the best

Feeling unhappy and overweight, Jane came to see me as
she felt very negative about her life. Seeing life as a glass half
empty, she spent her days trying to please her parents by
studying for more qualifications, all in an effort to be loved
by others. I taught Jane to start to love herself, to look within
and see the beauty inside her.

She started including the Butterfly Experience Affirmations in her life and soon she had set her goal to lose weight.
After some time learning to love herself, and appreciating
and getting to know the real person within, she transformed
herself from the inside out and lost over 28lb (12kg). She
learned to please herself and to say "No", something she had
found very hard to do. Her life totally turned around. Today,

she wears clothes that make her feel good, has an amazing social life, no longer needs to study obsessively and enjoys the life she has. She now has an attitude of gratitude.

What Jane had to change was her way of thinking. Her life wasn't bad. It was her perception of her life that changed. As Anthony Robbins says, "When we are grateful, fear disappears and abundance appears."

I don't want *you* to waste years of your life. Time is a great healer, but we can help it along. Imagine your life without those negative feelings. What would that feel like? What sort of a person would you be without negative thoughts? If you could learn to shed these daily, what would stop you growing?

The next chapter looks at how you can get into that higher vibration each day, how you can eliminate the negatives that are blocking your happiness. If you keep doing that, day after day, it will become effortless.

You're learning to fly, remember? Well, the next chapter is where you learn how to lighten your being daily, so that you can take flight. Remember to practise your self-relaxation throughout the following stage. The next chapter holds a fabulous new Butterfly Experience technique, the most vital tool in the Caterpillar section. I call it the Red-X Technique.

CHAPTER EIGHT

The Red-X Technique

THE BOTTOM LINE IS THAT we make our own choices. We choose our own emotions and actions. And so we have to learn to control those choices. Our emotions are rooted in our thought life. Our minds cannot be empty for more than a few seconds; they automatically fill up with thoughts. These thoughts can either be positive or negative. Here's your choice, right now. Do you want to continue to dwell on your negative thoughts or do you want to learn to dismiss them?

This is not mumbo-jumbo. Learning to rid yourself of negative thinking in the now is the best gift that you can give yourself. It's life-altering, mind-blowing in its simplicity and possible for anyone, in any circumstances.

It's free and it's phenomenal. And it's based on a simple principle. Here it is: *we can control our thoughts*. We have over 60,000 thoughts each day, most of them recycled from the day before. If they stay in your head, they demand to be fed and nurtured. We need to acknowledge our negative thoughts, but not allow the body to hold on to them. If you really apply the Red-X Technique, your life will change radically and more quickly than you ever thought possible.

How to use the Red-X Technique

I have chosen as an example sitting your driving test with a positive outcome, but you can use the Red-X Technique for any situation in your life, such as interviews, examinations or simply to feel better.

Imagine it's the day of your driving test. You wake up and your first thought is, "I'll never pass. I'll probably get a tough examiner. I just know I'll fail." You haven't even got out of bed yet and already your day is a disaster! Let's change those thoughts.

- First of all, pick up on the signals that your body is giving you – headache, tension, sweaty palms, cramps in your tummy, restlessness.

- STOP THE NEGATIVE THOUGHT! Red-X it from your mind. Literally imagine a huge red X over the negative thought.

- Now turn the negative thought into a positive thought. Talk to yourself as if the test has already happened. (Remember, the subconscious mind doesn't know the difference between true and untrue.) Tell yourself, "I've passed my driving test!"

- Now go into the alpha state (see pages 24–5). Daydream. Rehearse the day ahead, imagining yourself taking your driving test in a positive and controlled manner. See the test in detail, visualizing the traffic and the manoeuvres. Watch yourself dealing with them, driving effortlessly and easily.

- Every time a negative thought tries to raise its ugly head, immediately Red-X it from your mind.

- See yourself passing with flying colours, being congratulated by the examiner. Feel the pressure of the examiner's handshake. Believe you will pass. Very quickly your mind will get the message. Your *attitude* to the impending test will be entirely different. Your body language will be different. Your positive thoughts will reward you with a feeling of calm and composure. And you will pass the test!

Apply the Red-X Technique to all your negative thinking. Get into the habit of monitoring your thoughts. Don't let negative ones get through. As soon as you catch yourself thinking negatively, Red-X that thought! Bad habits – and that's all negative thinking is – take around 21 days to be broken. Over time you will start to think in a more positive way. With a little perseverance you'll feel better, more relaxed and open. Then just watch the opportunities come your way.

"I hope my meeting goes well today." A standard thought. But your subconscious, which has been disappointed in the past, hears only doubt: "There's a chance I won't pull this

off." During the meeting your body language starts signal-
ling that doubt, displaying a lack of confidence. Instead,
Red-X the negative thought and say, "My meeting went
well today", as if it has already happened. The subconscious
mind doesn't know if that statement is true or false. When
you arrive for the meeting, your body already thinks you're
a success. You look and feel confident, happy and positive.
And your outcome is very different.

We replace our thoughts all the time. Imagine that you
are watching a film at the cinema. Suddenly, you think about
painting your bedroom blue. Chances are you can simply
dismiss the thought with no effort at all. It drifts away and
you bring your full attention back to the film. The difference
here is that we do it *consciously*. With time, dismissing your
negative thoughts using the Red-X Technique becomes just
as natural a process. It keeps us from emotional confusion,
from over-stimulating the mind.

Think of it as learning to drive. In the beginning everything seems so difficult and complicated. But in no time
you've learned to drive automatically, the slightest pressure
on the steering wheel keeping you on your chosen path.
That's how quickly we can learn to dispel negative thinking
once we start to see the benefits.

You can use the Red-X Technique to stop yourself
being sabotaged by the past as well. How often have you
walked away from a situation feeling aggrieved, the
injured party? What might the outcome have been with
a little courage, if you had Red-X'd your fear and asked
the questions you had wanted to ask. Or if you had used

the Red-X Technique to allow yourself to see through negative thoughts, to see the situation as it really was? What thoughts about your past have held you back, thoughts you should have Red-X'd out? What beliefs have made you doubt yourself, made you angry, prevented you from moving on? Write them down – all the petty grudges that have rankled. How has your thinking about them, perhaps decades on, impacted on your life? If you didn't have those negative beliefs, those grudges, how different would life feel? Now go through the list, Red-Xing out the negatives and turning all those thoughts around, so you learn a positive lesson from each of them.

We shape and reshape our lives every day depending on how we feel about ourselves and others. Every day we place limitations on ourselves, rehashing old stories, wasting energy on the negatives, instead of looking for positive solutions. Look at your list – see how long it is. See how its pattern weaves through your life. With a little practice Red-X becomes as automatic as flicking the indicator when driving. Detour to a positive thought, and straightaway you right your thinking. By controlling your thinking through the Red-X Technique, your life will change – within days or weeks. It's a simple equation – when you think happy thoughts you experience more happiness. It's a great gift. Imagine being able to switch off your inner critic, to instantly stop the thoughts that play over and over in your mind and rob you of energy. Stop negative thoughts as soon as you become aware of them, before they have a chance to grow. This technique requires persistence.

I've created a Butterfly Experience Seven-step Reminder for you. Its aim is to reinforce the Caterpillar stage techniques daily, until you have changed your mindset.

The Butterfly Experience Seven-step Reminder

1. Remember to do your self-relaxation (see pages 30–32) for 15 minutes every day.

2. Red-X out any negative thoughts or statements made to you by yourself or others, restating them to yourself in a positive way.

3. Remember to focus on what you want, not what you *don't* want.

4. Remember to do something every day that takes you closer to your day's goal.

5. Remember to praise yourself when you achieve your desired outcome for that day.

6. Remember to eat healthily to give yourself energy.

7. Remember to be patient and kind to yourself and be grateful for all the growth you have already experienced.

Follow the Butterfly Experience Seven-step Reminder every day for 30 days. If you forget, you must start all over again.

More food for positive thought

Now you should be starting to make real changes in your life. Here are some other principles of positive thinking that you can use to change your thinking around on a daily basis, while you are practising the Red-X Technique.

Start looking for the "magical" feeling of happy, healthy functioning. That's a complicated way of saying everything feels OK. No judgments, no wishing things were different. Simply accept reality. If you asked a hundred "happy" people the secret of their success, none would maintain that they never feel negative emotions or experience negative thoughts. But virtually all of them would tell you that even in the midst of their negativity they trust there is something better coming and that there are more important things happening than the negative feelings they are currently experiencing. For every problem there is always a solution.

No one avoids problems in life. In fact, the stress they bring can be good for us. The psychologist Carl Jung (1875–1961) said, "Man needs difficulties: they are necessary for health." Meeting and overcoming challenges is a source of psychological well-being.

Once you begin to recognize healthy thinking it will become vital to your peace of mind. Discovering *your* level of healthy functioning is all you need to live a genuinely happy, productive life. Healthy, positive thinking will outweigh any source of misery. This process involves learning self-awareness – in other words, no more denying how you feel. Accept your emotions honestly, and learn which ones work for you and which work against you.

CHAPTER NINE

F.E.A.R.

WHICH EMOTION IS MOST counterproductive to our happiness? Which is the most important instar we face as we go through the Caterpillar stage of the Butterfly Experience? *Fear!*

Over the years clients have come to me with every possible condition. I've been asked to improve fertility, and to help with multiple sclerosis, almost all types of cancer and every form of anxiety. I have also helped to alleviate the discomfort of terminal illness. Fear is our biggest enemy – it is the enemy within.

Fear stops us growing. It makes us live small lives. Fear is learned behaviour – we are not born with it. Negative experiences in childhood mean that from an early age we stop trusting. We become more self-reliant in an effort to save ourselves pain. From being infants who trust everyone, we go on to fear everything but our own instincts. But being human we err, we let ourselves down. Now we know our own limitations. And so we begin to buy into fear.

Fearful thoughts, allowed to grow, become real. We make them real. We feed them and keep them alive. We associate, imbuing current situations with painful memories. We catastrophize our thinking until disaster lurks around every corner and our thoughts are like newspaper headlines. Our confidence disappears. And with our confidence goes opportunity. How often have you wanted to try something new, but run away from it? How often have you wanted to speak to someone and walked away? What has fear cost you up until now?

Yet those of us living life free from fear understand that fear is just an illusion. I have a neat acronym: F.E.A.R., standing for "False Emotions Appearing Real". Fear is ugly, paralyzing and corrosive. I want to show you how to turn fear around so that it becomes a gift, a signal from your body to change things for the better.

Remember Pavlov's dog? The Russian scientist Ivan Pavlov (1849–1936) discovered that when he rang a bell before feeding his dogs, they would start to salivate. After a while he rang the bell and offered no food, yet the dogs still salivated. Pavlov realized that salivating was a conditioned response. The dogs had *assumed* that the dinner would be there.

Fear is a conditioned response. When you are fearful, you are assuming certain things about yourself, your abilities and limitations. Become aware of this conditioned response through your body's signals – the racing heart, the sweaty palms. We react in that way because we have been *programmed* to do so. Once you have mastered the Red-X Technique of eliminating negative thoughts you can go on to the next level. You can begin to break down these fearful assumptions – identify them, name them, accept them. The next step is to change your reaction to them. That's freedom. By being willing to try again, to look at things differently, we learn new thinking, new behaviours.

Take a few minutes to sit and think about your own fears and anxieties. Be honest. A little bit of soul surgery is required here, so dig deep. Put the book down and come back to it when you're ready. This can be sore – we like to think of ourselves as brave. But identifying these stumbling blocks is the first step to eradicating them. And once you've learned how to do the exercise below, it's such a healing feeling knowing you have a way to …

Overcome fear

Take a few moments to try the following visualization exercise to help you let go of fear and anxiety.

1. Sit in a comfortable position with your back straight. Allow your eyes to close and mentally count down from ten to one.

2. Allow yourself to float off to your favourite place where you feel safe and secure. Spend a little time identifying what it is you are currently afraid of. Is it:

   • Fear of dying?

   • Fear of loss?

   • Fear of failure?

   • Fear of being found out?

   Name the fears and the price you have paid.

3. Breathing easily, see yourself facing each fear. Look at yourself as if on a screen. Using your new ability to see things differently, understand that you have created this fear. See how your negative thinking has fed it. Own up to any part you have played in it.

4. Sometimes fear comes as a result of guilt (because we are ashamed of our actions). Spend time with your Higher Self, feeling grateful for any realizations.

5. Visualize the fears. Watch yourself putting all these fears into a pink balloon. Tie a knot in the balloon and send it skyward. Take a deep breath, blowing out any residue of fear. Say:

**I am willing and open to allowing any fears
or anxieties to be released from my life.**

6. Inhale deeply. Imagine you are breathing in pure, inspiring energy. Surround your body with a white light of confidence and happiness. Feel this light pervade your whole body, through every cell and muscle.

7. Bring your mind back to the room. Count up from one to ten, opening your eyes at the count of eight, feeling wide awake.

After completing the exercise you will feel that your body and mind are completely clear of any fears and anxieties. Continue to do this exercise every day for one week, as reinforcement.

CHAPTER TEN

Seven Further Instars for Growth

T HE TWO VITAL TECHNIQUES – Red-X and F.E.A.R. – explained in Chapters Eight and Nine will catapult you to a better life. And that's not all. Here are some more wonderful Caterpillar stage tips to develop your spirit and emotions. Remember the instars mentioned in Chapter Six? The caterpillar goes through a number of radical transformations, each time shedding its skin to reveal an exciting new undercoat. The following seven Instar Lessons will help you progress through the Caterpillar stage.

Instar One: Look for the positive

We are so conditioned to think in a negative way that we search for negatives that don't exist. Have you ever gone for an interview telling yourself that you won't get the job? And then not been surprised when the prophecy fulfils itself? Think in a positive manner at all times. It will shine through. There is always a solution to any problem – you just have to look for it.

This applies even when life takes a serious turn for the worse. Often it's only a drastic situation that really makes you sit up and think. Say you've been made redundant from work. The negative approach would be to find plenty of things to worry about – bills to pay, the loss of status. What about the opportunities that have just been handed to you, such as finding a job that suits you better, one that will make you feel happier? See every problem as a challenge, a chance to change and step out of your comfort zone.

Instar Two: Stay away from negative thinkers

Misery loves company. Negative people are a magnet for other negative people. If your friends are downbeat, then it's time to change who you spend your time with. Start thinking in a more positive manner and just watch the wonderful people you attract – vibrant, energetic, happy people who want the best for others.

Instar Three: Stop trying to control everything

Connect to the universe every day. I can't stress enough the importance of our connection to Spirit. It's the source of all things for me. You may be sceptical but I'm just asking you to *try* it. There's a whole chapter later on about spirituality (see pages 242–7), our need for it and how to access it in your life. But today, just ask for help, especially if times are difficult. That's when you need it most. Ask Spirit to give you the courage and strength to go on. Ask it to lift your mood if you're feeling low. And if things are going well, ask it to direct you toward others you can help, and be grateful.

Instar Four: Be in the now

Your past is just a figment of your imagination; the future is a projection of the same. The only moment that is real is RIGHT NOW. Live it with passion, live it honourably, live it honestly. Learning to trust yourself is not as difficult as you may think. Next time you have to make a decision, mentally ask your body for a sign. First ask it the question and then *feel* how your body reacts. Some people feel it in their chest; I feel my body's response in my gut. I literally "go with my gut" for all decisions. The more you practise this vital skill, the healthier your thinking will be. The more often your body shows you the way forward, the more you will come to rely on it. Your ego may lie to you. Your body never does. Be proud of who you are.

Instar Five: Be yourself

Work at changing your own mindset, not the thinking of others. No two people are the same. Even identical twins have their own fingerprints. Have you noticed that although identical twins have such similar personalities, one is always slightly happier, the other slightly sadder? It's like two sides of the same coin. Yet we all try to make others think and act like us. The truth is, we are meant to have our individual ideas and beliefs. We need to be different because we all have a unique purpose and destiny. Use your precious energy to find your purpose, instead of wasting it by comparing yourself to others.

Instar Six: Stand up for yourself

Think of people you know who try to control other people's lives. Why do they act in that domineering and manipulative (even bullying) way? The truth is that they are trying to control their environment because *their own emotions are out of control*. They need to learn to relax, to let go and accept others as they are. Stand up for yourself. Don't put up with unacceptable behaviour. Don't be a doormat. Bullies sense a victim a mile away. Be yourself. Speak your truth. Others don't have to agree, but being true to yourself will win you respect.

Instar Seven: Have fun

Work at creating sunshine in your life. Without fun and laughter life is a drudge. We all know individuals who moan constantly. Get proactive about your own happiness. Stop right now and decide one thing that you will do to brighten up your day. Meet an old friend. Buy yourself some fresh flowers. Take a walk in the park. Paint a picture without worrying about how it looks. Watch a favourite movie. *Remember to smile.* It helps your heart stay happy. Be kind to others, but remember to be kind to yourself, too. Share your life with other people. Celebrate!

Focusing energy

Below I've given you seven tasks to help you focus on some energy fundamentals for this section. From today I want you to practise them, becoming more aware of your energy and the energy of others.

Task One

Every day, spend some time focusing on what you want to happen. Use positive thinking every day to see the outcomes you want in life. Bring them alive, so your subconscious feels as though these good things have already happened.

Task Two

Remember to protect yourself against negative people. One head teacher of a school told me that he thought of his staff as "radiators" and "drainers". He simply meant that some people's energy is boiling hot – you can feel it. Then there are the others we all know – the ones who suck us dry. These are the people who make us feel tired at the end of the day, drained of energy. Be aware of the energy around you. Avoid reading newspapers filled with toxic stories and watching rubbish on the television.

Task Three

Make a conscious decision to only be around positive people. Surround yourself with positive energy. Read positive books and listen to upbeat music that will lift your vibrations. Seek the good in other people and believe that everyone is doing their best. But give yourself permission to move away from people who vex your spirit. This section is all about energy. It is so important that we protect ourselves from negative energy. You would keep your distance from someone who had a bad cold and was coughing, so why would you allow other people's negative energy to surround you?

Task Four

Be aware of your body language and how it can affect others. We wear our pain on the outside and people pick up on it. "Fake it to make it" until your improved thinking automatically improves the way your are around others. When you believe in yourself, you radiate confidence.

Task Five

Lay a good foundation for growth by staying within your natural character – don't try to become a clone of anyone else. Embrace your gifts and work on building up your confidence. Stop trying to "read" other people's thoughts. You are responsible only for your own.

Task Six

Never give up and always believe in your dream. Persistence is the key to success in all areas of life. There is always a solution; you just have to find it. Get creative. Open yourself up to new ideas.

Task Seven

Never accept "No" for an answer. Always try, try and try again. The British entrepreneur Sir Richard Branson says that although he listens with care to others, he still relies on himself and makes up his own mind. "To thine own self be true." (William Shakespeare, *Hamlet*.)

Now that you understand the process, you can practise daily and grow daily. But how do you use the Butterfly Experience to move to the next level of emotional, financial and spiritual security?

It's time to ask what clarity you have in your life. Is your vision hazy or is it very clear? Do you know exactly what you desire and how to achieve it? Do you truly believe it will happen?

Let's get you there, by using the "Three Cs" of the Caterpillar stage.

CHAPTER ELEVEN

Trusting the Three Cs

The Three Cs are:

Commitment

Courage

Control

We make a *commitment* to move forward in life.

We have the *courage* to take that next step.

We stay in *control* of our lives.

Commitment

The Dalai Lama, giving advice for meditation, states, "… in your life, unless you make specific time for something that you feel committed to, you will always have other obligations and you will always be too busy."

To be truly successful at anything, you need commitment. Commitment isn't something you can pretend to have, because you'll soon be found out. Commitment comes through belief. Make a commitment today to visualize regularly the new, more positive YOU. Make a commitment to dream of the success that's headed your way. Make a commitment to bin the old plan, the one where you just waited for something to happen. Make a commitment to spend real time and invest real energy in deciding what you want from life.

Committing to a goal often means making sacrifices. It sometimes means admitting that the old way we've been doing things hasn't worked. It means looking for new strategies. Keep your mind focused on what's important. Set your goals. Prioritize and be realistic about what you can achieve. Visualize what you want to do and visualize yourself doing it.

Commit to your happiness, to finding and following your true purpose. Each and every sacrifice will be worth it. Unless we commit ourselves to focusing on something that fulfils us, life can just seem to pass us by. We waste our lives waiting for them to start. Commit daily to what you are trying to achieve. When you do, you'll be rewarded. And that's a feeling you can't buy.

There are those in life who make things happen, those who watch things happen and those who say, "What happened?" You can sit around admiring the beautiful butterfly. Or you can start today to make changes so that you can become a butterfly, too.

Courage

There are examples of courage all around us – from children with terminal illnesses to whole nations showing tremendous bravery. It's necessary to recognize that living the life you're destined to live will take a little courage.

Courage involves self-awareness, being honest with yourself. It means stepping out of your comfort zone, remembering that you can always return there if you have to. When we've found the courage to take the first, difficult step, most of us discover how fantastic it feels to stretch ourselves and to experience living in the moment.

How much courage do you have in your current mindset? I want you to go within yourself, right now, and ask yourself that question. Ask yourself, how free do you want to be? How small does your life have to get before you can find it within yourself to break out of that prison you've made? Do you have enough courage to start thinking positively? DO IT NOW. What is it that holds you back? Ask yourself and be prepared and willing to name it. By admitting the truth you can acknowledge it and let it go.

Control

Here's one of the great paradoxes of positive thinking – in order to be in control of our lives, we have to relinquish control. The need for control is negative thinking – it's damage limitation. This need is an insidious weed. When you eradicate it, your life will be calmer, happier and healthier.

Why is it that people are so afraid to let go? In my

practice, I see people with control issues time and time again. Often clients are unwilling to admit their controlling behaviour or else are totally unaware of it. Many of my clients have responsible positions – as psychiatrists, physicians, nurses, teachers, managers and lawyers. They come to see me because they are stressed and they are horrified when I tell them that they've created the stress themselves by trying to control others. When they learn to control their own thoughts and emotions, they take back control of their life. There is less stress and anxiety. They learn to relax.

This alone gives us a tremendous feeling of security and happiness. Releasing negative thoughts about others frees us. It allows us to devote time to what we want in life, and how to achieve it. It is our birthright to be happy. When we let go of our fears and stop trying to control others we become happier.

If you can admit that life is not what you would like it to be, that in itself is a start. It is the *beginning* of a new way of thinking. Carrying around negative thoughts about others makes us unhappy and dispirited. Can you imagine letting go of your negative thoughts? Can you imagine not caring how others perceive you? Well, you can be like this! You can release your anxieties. Your mind becomes lighter and clearer. Now you can go forward with confidence.

Having gone through the process of shedding, let's focus now on what you need to take you beyond this stage. Remember that the Caterpillar stage is all about learning and growing, and fearlessly getting rid of some bad habits. To help you do this, the next pages focus on some life-changing techniques that you can bring into your life easily and effectively.

Body language techniques

Here are some proven techniques for making a good first impression – often overlooked and so easy to rectify. By becoming more aware of your own body language, and also by recognizing the body language of others, you can develop your own self-esteem and change how others think about you. People naturally want to know what kind of a person they are dealing with. You might feel your speech tells them that, but your body language gives out far more information. From it they know if you're confident or insecure, quiet or extrovert. Whether you're the kind of person people listen to.

We all interpret body language all the time on a sub-conscious level. We start forming impressions of people we meet from the moment we set eyes on them. A huge part of the first impression you create comes from your posture, facial expression, eye contact and gestures. This body language speaks louder than anything you say.

It's vital to use your energy to make a positive impression. Even if you feel like a marshmallow inside. So hold your back straight and your head up, and dress in a confident way. Neat and tidy hair is a must, as is a welcoming smile. These simple things go a long way to making you look positive, even if you don't feel it. The secret is in looking confident. By looking confident you will start to act and behave in that way. Others will respect you.

To help your body language, work on your self-belief. In the morning take a few precious minutes to affirm positive Butterfly Experience Affirmations about your-

self. As you say them you are retraining your mind.
For example:

I believe I am powerful.

I believe I am successful.

I believe I am confident.

Try it and see the difference!

Body Language Giveaways

Your face is the most easy-to-read part of your body.
Your expression can make you look bored or animated,
interested or frankly turned off. Make a conscious
effort to smile at people. Being able to smile easily
and warmly is a simple gift you can give yourself.
Focus on your smile over the next few days, especially
when meeting new people. Your smile is one of the
strongest tools you have. It makes you look friendly,
open and warm.

Your eyes tell people how you're really feeling – it's
hard to hide your emotions if you give eye contact.
That's the reason why people like it and why
they distrust those who find eye contact difficult.
They want to know what you're hiding. Making
very little eye contact can also convey shyness or

►

submissiveness. Don't overcompensate, though, as a direct stare can be very intimidating – it implies intensity. Aim for the middle ground – holding people's eyes for a short while to tell them that you are at ease. Direct eye contact is of the utmost importance. It builds trust.

Your hands also express the inner you. Fidgeting makes everyone aware of how nervous you are feeling. Constantly touching your clothes or face can make you look anxious and even false. Try to use open gestures – they show honesty. But keep them moderate. You can express enthusiasm and commitment without knocking over vases. Big gestures make you appear out of control. Pay attention to your handshake – it should be firm and neither too hard nor too soft. Power handshakes are to be avoided – people instinctively know that you are trying to dominate from the onset.

Your posture conveys your level of self-confidence. When we are less than assured we hunch our shoulders. Even if you feel nervous, push those shoulders back and try to adopt a more upright stance.

Your position relative to other people is also important. Turn toward people as you are speaking to them. People who are paying attention lean slightly

➤

forward. Leaning backward demonstrates aloofness or rejection. Standing too far away seems standoffish. Try to judge people's personal space correctly – it's easy to overstep the mark and intimidate people.

In summary, our body language betrays what's happening inside us. Being aware of our body language lets us send out good messages about ourselves and raises our self-confidence.

Caterpillar colours

In this Caterpillar phase I want you to become aware of the colours that you wear and the colours in your environment. Colours are important – changing them is an easy way to change the way you feel. Each colour has its own energetic wavelength and frequency. Subconsciously we pick up on colour messages all the time. The box opposite gives a short summary of how colours can affect our mood and the mood of those around us. Caterpillars use colours to advantage. Some caterpillars become progressively brighter as they go through each instar, perhaps as a signal that they are changing. You, too, have the ability to change with each insight and realization, so try out new colours. Show people that you are changing.

Try using colour energy boosts along with my suggestions for improved body language. But beware: none of these changes can disguise a poor attitude.

Colours for Every Mood

Red helps to assert authority. It will make you feel confident and give you an energy boost. This passionate colour is said to be the colour of love, and it helps to stimulate your heartbeat. Use red in your home to manifest abundance. Wearing it makes you look vital, alive.

Green helps you to concentrate and be more focused. This is one of the most popular colours for people's homes. It is very calming and helps focus and vision. Wearing green makes others think you are friendly, a team player and well balanced.

Blue calms you in times of stress. Wear it if you want to look or feel serene – the body will respond by actually producing calming chemicals. By looking at the colour blue you stimulate the thyroid and that affects your heart, bones, hair and reproductive organs. Verbal ability is also improved when you wear blue. If you're involved in negotiations, wear navy – it makes you look trustworthy.

Purple is a good intellect booster, so great when you need to do some brainstorming. It is said to be a romantic and feminine colour. Purple helps you be more intuitive and connects you to a Higher Consciousness. Wearing purple makes you look ethical and high-minded.

►

Yellow is cheerful. People who wear it are considered optimists. Think of spring and daffodils. Yellow enhances concentration. Wear it if you need to do analytical work. It is said to be a holistic colour.

Orange is a hot, vibrant and spicy colour. If you want to stand out in a room, wear orange. For many, orange is the colour of happiness. It promotes energy and focus. Orange makes you look enthusiastic about life.

Gold is linked with the sun and masculine power.

Silver is associated with the moon and denotes feminine energy.

Attitude

How *is* your attitude? Be completely honest now. Rate yourself out of ten. Do you stomp around at work moaning all day? Do people tip-toe around your moods? Or do people describe you as a ray of sunshine or a breath of fresh air? Perhaps you are somewhere in between.

In the Caterpillar stage your sole task is to grow. Start thinking today about your attitude to family and work. What you put into life you'll get back tenfold. Do you pull your weight at work, or sit back waiting for some other fool to volunteer? Do you act as though the world owes you a living?

The best way I know to improve attitude is self-acceptance. Accept yourself the way you are, and work to improve what you feel would advance you. Peace of mind comes from knowing we've done our best. The only approval that matters is approval of ourselves. We don't need praise from others to make us happy. When you believe in yourself you give off a positive self-image. Just by looking at you, people know you have clear ideas and know where you are going in life. You stand out.

Attitude shows most keenly when we're challenged. I recently met someone who had just been made redundant. He was positively radiant, happy to have been given an opportunity to start investing in another company. He had put all his energy into this new venture. Think of a challenging time in *your* life. Think how you handled it. Would you do the same today? No – of course you wouldn't. We learn and we *grow*. When we feel good about who we are we can look at life's difficulties in different ways.

When we have a positive attitude we are halfway to achieving our goals. We feel and look better, we are more confident and happier with ourselves. The strong, confident person sees an obstacle in a challenging way, looking for new opportunities to grow. Caterpillars can fall off a leaf many times, but they always climb back up again.

Sir Tom Hunter, the millionaire Scottish entrepreneur, says: "We have opportunities every day of our lives; it's knowing which ones will make us successful." I have always looked at challenges as new opportunities. There is always a solution in every problem – we just need to look for and be open to it. Have an air of expectancy about you, look for great things to happen.

CHAPTER TWELVE

Caterpillar Self-care

OFTEN, SOME OF THE THINGS that we most dislike about ourselves are the unhealthy habits we indulge in. The caterpillar stage is where you shed these – stopping smoking for example, or dumping the idea that you don't need to exercise.

By changing the way you think, you'll begin to look fabulous on the outside. Caterpillars know that things are good in moderation. Having a glass of wine with your meal is acceptable, but often one glass leads to two or three. At first you may feel relaxed, but if you continue to drink, you'll probably start to get moody. Before you know it the bottle is empty. Don't over-indulge in alcohol. It leaves the body feeling low and depressed. Alcohol, like all drugs, is a toxin. The same goes for smoking. People who smoke have a tougher skin surface. Their fingers are stained yellow. Imagine the damage they are doing on the inside.

Caterpillars know that avoiding harmful substances is the only way to live a long and healthy life.

TAKE A MOMENT TO THINK ABOUT

HOW YOU TREAT YOUR BODY.

What age do you feel? What age are you really? Do they match? Poor diet, lack of exercise and fresh air – for so long your body has accepted mental and physical abuse, all self-imposed. The Caterpillar stage is where we say we're no longer going to accept the way we've been treating ourselves. You wouldn't treat a child that way, so why do it to yourself?

Butterfly Energy

Your Butterfly Experience Blueprint (see pages 199–208) is determined to a degree by the body you have and how you look after it. This section will discuss possible problems and offer a prescription for health. I believe that we have the ability to heal ourselves. So I want to help you get in touch with your Butterfly Energy.

Everything in life is energy. The world is energy. We are energy; our food, our possessions, the plants that surround us are all energy. Energy is all around us. Think of the ocean, that vast electric bath. Full of powerful energy and yet we can be soothed and relaxed by listening to the waves lapping to and fro. Energy is within us, too. You know the energy you love to feel inside when you are preparing to go on holiday? You are on a high and feel wonderful. Or the energy you feel at a concert when your favourite band is playing? The energy is electric. That's the feel-good factor we get when we harness this energy. We all have the power within us to choose and create our own life.

As the poet Tennyson (1809–1892) said, "I am part of all that I have met." We all live in a huge energy field. Where does our energy come from? We take it in through food and the air around us, and also from other people. The Dalai Lama is small in stature, but his magnificent, wonderful energy is tangible. When he walks into a room, you can *feel* his joy. Despite all the sorrow and injustice he has encountered, he remains compassionate and resilient. He has never forgotten his life purpose – to serve others. These qualities have made him one of the greatest spiritual leaders in the world today.

Not everyone controls their energy so well. Intuitively, we pick up on emotional signals, almost without being aware of it. We avoid certain people instinctively. When someone comes too close and steps into "our space", we feel their energy. Some people we trust naturally. Others repel us - we feel their tension immediately. Why is that? It's their energy. Can you think of a time you went for an interview? Relive that moment and feel the energy in the room. Either it felt relaxed or it felt unpleasant. That feeling came from the people in their room. It was their energy. We all know someone who makes us feel low, lacking in confidence, who makes us feel drained. Our energy seeps out to them. You can particularly feel someone's fear or anger, if that is the energy they are giving out. We pick up on energy. Sense it. Others do too – when we feel sad or below par, our friends and family notice. We give out a different energy.

When we are swimming against the universal energy flow, things go from bad to worse. We've all had those days. We oversleep, then every traffic light turns red, then nothing goes right at work … Instead, this invisible energy should help us to live our life. We have to learn to trust in the process of life, to flow with the universal energy. *Anything can happen if we let it.* If we think in a positive manner, our energy changes. We attract people with the same vibrations. When our energy is up, everything seems fine. Success keeps on bringing success. Things always go right. Opportunities arise and unusual events occur. So why not learn to tune into energy, work with it, benefit from it?

Self-healing

For thousands of years humans have been aware of the holistic health benefits of working with healing energy. Energy is all around us. Think of the electricity that comes from water, the sheer power of it. Envisage the energy that goes into delivering a baby. Remember the energy of a wedding day, the joy that was created around the happy couple. Energy is a wonderful tool, but it must be used wisely.

It doesn't matter what our religion or cultural background is, we all have the ability to use our own healing energy, balancing the subtle vibrations within and around our bodies. The medical profession has started to become more open to this concept. If we have an imbalance in our bodies, then our energies are out of alignment. The solution is simple. We need to listen to our bodies, to communicate with them. But most of us are so reliant on medication and intervention that we have forgotten how to read the body's signals.

Where do these imbalances come from? Over a lifetime we accumulate so much baggage. Most of us should have a removal truck following us around – Regrets R Us. The sad part is that we cling on to all those negative beliefs that we have collected about ourselves and our family, friends and society. This negative energy is what creates the imbalances in our energy field, causing illness and disease.

Neither fame nor wealth nor talent makes us immune to negative energy. The actress Judy Garland had the most wonderful singing voice. She was born to entertain. Her energy lit up the stage. Sadly, the wonderful energy she had as a child began to change. Judy seemed to attract the wrong partners and her problems included alcohol dependency and physical abuse. Judy's life, which started out so full of promise, spiralled deeper into despair. Photographs and film footage of her in her later years are so sad – her energy was sending out a signal for help. Aged 47 she died from barbiturate poisoning. The coroner's verdict was accidental death. I believe she died of a broken spirit.

The good news is that generating negative energy is a habit that can be unlearned. As with self-relaxation, we can learn new skills and techniques – such as my Chakra Meditation to rebalance your energy (see pages 109–10). This is true for all of us, no matter how low we've been. We are all energy channels. That means that we can heal our own bodies. I have witnessed so many examples of people healing themselves using their own energy, self-belief and determination to live. And I want to teach you to do the same.

Kundalini

According to Eastern tradition, the body has seven energy centres known as "chakras" ("chakra" is Sanskrit for "wheel"). These regulate the flow of energy through our energy system, opening and closing when we think and feel. When we practise self-relaxation or meditation, we access our power to self-heal by tapping into our kundalini energy. This is our life force, the energy in our spirit body, known in India as *prana*, in China as *chi* and in Japan as *ki*. Kundalini energy lies inside our root chakra (the word "kundalini" means "coiled up like a snake" in Sanskrit), with the potential to rise right up to our crown chakra. When this kundalini energy flows through our body, we feel re-energized, calmer and more positive.

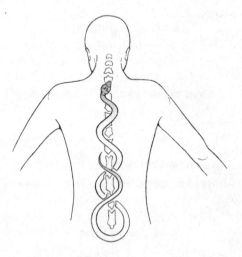

Kundalini rising

The chakras

Each of the seven major chakras is associated with a
particular colour and represents a different ability:

✦

Crown chakra (seventh chakra) – white
Ability to connect to your spirituality

✦

Third eye chakra (sixth) – purple
Ability to open up to create your vision of the future

✦

Throat chakra (fifth) – blue
Ability to communicate

✦

Heart chakra (fourth) – green
Ability to love

✦

Solar plexus chakra (third) – yellow
Ability to be in control of your life

✦

Sacral chakra (second) – orange
Ability to accept change and new experiences

✦

Root chakra (first) – red
Ability to be grounded in life

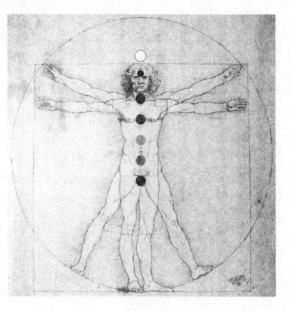

The chakras

Chakra Meditation

This meditation can be used for awakening the conscious mind. By focusing on the seven major chakras, or energy centres, we can learn to balance the flow of energy throughout the body.

1. Sit comfortably in a chair with your back straight and your head supported. Focus on your breathing and listen to your heartbeat.

2. Start to focus on the crown chakra, just above the top of your head. Allow its white colour to melt down gently through your body.

3. Bring your attention down to your "third eye" chakra. Let its purple colour blend with the white and allow your focus to be drawn farther down your body.

4. Focus on your throat chakra and allow its healing blue colour to melt through your body, starting to replenish any parts of your body that feel tired.

5. Allow the energy to continue down into your heart chakra, and let its beautiful green colour circle around your heart to fill your body with peace and contentment.

6. Be aware of your body beginning to relax more and more as you go deeper into this wonderful meditation.

7. Focus on your solar plexus chakra, and feel the warmth of its yellow colour, warm and soft like the sun.

8. Now that you have reached your sacral chakra, envisage a beautiful bright orange colour. Let it circulate all around, healing your body with its natural energy.

9. You are now at your root chakra, which grounds your whole body. This chakra has a bright red colour. Allow your body to just be for a few moments and enjoy all the colours blending with your own energy and Spirit energy. Let the body bask for a few moments in the beautiful, blissful feeling of emptiness and of just letting go. This is the most precious time for your body. It is re-energizing itself, restoring and rebalancing and learning to just be.

10. When you are ready, allow yourself to be fully awake and in the present. Feel the difference in your body.

Caterpillars often have to deal with many problems simultaneously. In the Caterpillar stage, you may feel that you still have many obstacles to overcome. You've made a tremendous start by recognizing negative thinking patterns. Now I want you to consider some external forces that will try to steal your peace of mind. Before entering the chrysalis stage, most caterpillars enter a searching, wandering period. This final journey is often the most dangerous. It is important to be able to connect to source energy. We all look to one another to help us, but who do we trust? By connecting to source energy, you will start to build trust in yourself and others. The world is a beautiful place, but it can also be very frightening. Be aware of how you think, who your friends are, and who you can trust. Can you trust yourself? You are building your inner resources for the future, to help you through your life. Because the world is full of …

Predators

Constantly on the hunt for nourishment, driven by the need to grow, caterpillars use their natural gifts to avoid attack. They are careful, aware of the predators around them. Some develop colourings that allow them to blend in. Still, every excursion for nourishment is a trade-off between satisfying their hunger and facing potential dangers.

Predators are drawn by contrast or movement. By now you should feel yourself moving, see yourself changing – and you might already seem different to other people. This might mean that people around you are trying to stop you changing and growing. Luckily, hunger for life has allowed caterpillars to develop a key skill – the ability to distinguish chemical signatures. In other words, they know what to avoid. We, too, have to learn whom to avoid. And how. We all know people who are hyper-stressed. They lurch from one crisis to the next, nervous and bad-tempered. No matter what the situation, they look at it negatively, seeing problems as unsolvable. Unhappy, they insist on sharing their unhappiness with others. Some even resort to anger or bullying other people. Does this sound familiar?

Caterpillars sometimes wander away from their known environment, to be safe and survive. Their environment may no longer offer them enough to grow, and in the last stages of growth they may seek new territory. Are your needs being met where you are? Or do you need to make a move?

People who are *in control* of their lives are high-energy people, motivated, constantly eager to learn and grow. You need to be in control. When you believe in the process of life, that everything happens for a purpose, then uncanny events start to happen. Every day we are faced with different challenges. The real difference -- the road less travelled – is in how we deal with them. So let's talk a little about …

Protective energy

Are you calm, focused and positive? Or are you sending out stress signals and negative energy? Perhaps the changes that you've experienced by now are making you "stick out" a little. That might make you feel vulnerable.

Do you ever meet or work with people who drain you of energy? When you are connecting to source through self-relaxation or meditation, your energy shield is opened up through your chakra system. When you have completed your spiritual time with source energy, you must close yourself down. Just imagine a door closing or a lily flower closing up. Or simply say in your mind, "I am closing myself up now."

It is extremely important to do this, otherwise you are wide open to people stealing your energy. People will recognize if your energy levels are up and your vibration is raised. You will stand out in the crowd. People love energy people and always want to be around them. They are drawn to their positive, upbeat energy. Just be careful that you don't give your energy away and are left drained.

Each morning while getting dressed after my shower, I mentally put on a blue velvet cloak. I do this to protect myself from other people's negative energy, in order to avoid becoming drained. I only take off my cloak when I retire to bed. It's important to keep it on mentally – even with your own family. They, too, can have problems and negativity. You can choose a blue velvet cloak like mine, or imagine a glass jar over your body. Some people prefer to think of an aura of golden light surrounding their body as protection.

Managing stress

How stressed are you? We all need a certain amount of stress to feel good, but too much stress can and will affect your health, literally making you *distressed*. Stress manifests itself in so many ways, physically and emotionally. When we think of stress, we tend to think of going for interviews, bereavement, moving house or too much work. But stress affects us every day, in dozens of minor ways. Its compound effect is devastating. Most of us are subject to emotional stress without even knowing it. So before you have a break-down on your way to work, you need to recognize stress and deal with it. Each person has a unique experience of stress. When you understand stress and how it affects your life, you can choose to lead a healthier lifestyle and take pre-cautions against it.

How is your energy level, right now, this minute?

- Do you wake up each day with a smile on your face, ready for the new day ahead? Or do you wish you could go back to bed?

- Do you seek a solution for every problem? Or do you give up, finding life too hard?

- Do you run out of energy halfway through every race?

- Do you hate confrontation and avoid difficult conversations, either in the boardroom or at home?

- Do you avoid making decisions, for fear of making the wrong one?

Begin the process of change with a decision. Start *now*. Decide to find the time to heal yourself. Decide what needs to change in order to get rid of any imbalances you have created over the years. To grow we need constant change.

The secret is believing that change doesn't have to be stressful. It can be as easy or as hard as you like. You decide. You're in control.

Think about losing weight, for example. At first we feel out of our comfort zone. Then people compliment us and tell us that we look great. We start to feel good and act in a confident manner. Now we feel fantastic and wonder how we could have allowed that weight to remain. It is remarkable just how quickly we adjust to change.

Think again about what you want to change – something that will challenge you and take you out of your comfort zone. Do you want to change your shape? Your look? No matter what changes you make, at first you will feel awkward. But very quickly self-acceptance creeps in. Notice how quickly you feel in control and fabulous.

Eating habits

Caterpillars are eating machines, devouring everything in their path that will help them move through the process as quickly as possible. They can grow quickly or slowly, depending on how fast they get hold of what they need. As they wander from place to place in search of food, they are also looking for a safe spot to begin the next phase in their transformation.

It is vital that we nourish ourselves well during the Caterpillar stage of the Butterfly Experience. How can we feel energetic and glow with health on the outside if our bodies are full of rubbish inside?

Do you comfort eat to get through life? The body needs constant repair. Like a car, it breaks down if you don't look after it. Fill a car up with the wrong petrol and you get "kangaroo jumps". If you fill up your body with the wrong food, you also get a bad reaction. Nutrition is key to your well-being, physical and mental. You have to nourish yourself with healthy food. Otherwise your body and mind will become run down and finally break down.

Nutrition plays an important role in healing. When I see clients, the first thing I often ask them to do is detoxify their body. We look at foods that will increase energy and restore the body to a more alkaline base. Once the physical is taken care of, we move toward the mental and emotional side of their healing. In my experience, no matter what problem clients present with, if they improve their mindset about nutrition, every aspect of their health improves.

People forget that sometimes food isn't there simply for our pleasure. Food is nourishment. It's a necessity for our physical well-being. The quality of our food has an immediate impact on our health. If a car can't run without petrol, why do we think our body can be energized with no food or the wrong kind of food? When we feed our body the right food we feel stronger. Our mood improves – we are less irritable as we benefit from better digestion. We have enough energy to achieve our goals.

> *Not what we have but what we enjoy*
> *constitutes abundance.*
>
> EPICURUS (341–270 BCE)

Forget fad diets. For most of us, eating well is a far greater priority. Instead of resorting to high-sugar snacks that give us a false sense of energy, think nutrition. With a little thought and a positive mindset, turning our diet around can make all the difference between low energy and the quality of life we're aiming for. Love your body. Eat well. Eat everything in moderation. You'll soon see the difference.

You have to assess what you are feeding your body on a daily basis. Avoid sugary snacks as sugar stimulates the brain chemical beta endorphin. This is the same brain chemical that is affected by morphine and heroin. Sugar gives us a feeling of euphoria and wellness that soon wears off, leaving us angry and irritable. This is withdrawal. If you take more sugar, it will relieve your negative feelings – but the cycle continues. Sugar tricks the brain into thinking it is alleviating these symptoms. In fact, it makes you feel worse.

Sugar turns into fat. We pile on the weight thinking those chocolate bars are helping relieve our pain. What we need is to be in control of our emotions. Sugar makes them out of control. Ditto the caffeine we drink every day. Everything in moderation. Instead of a cup of coffee, which becomes a crutch, start your day with a healthy fruit juice. Coffee often causes a drastic "gut reaction". Your body doesn't lie. It knows which foods and substances are bad for it. Listen to what it's telling you.

The freshly hatched caterpillar is very soft and vulnerable. So caterpillars are careful what they feed their bodies. Good food is made up of different types of nutrients, including vitamins and minerals as well as a balance of protein, carbohydrate and fat.

Essential vitamins and minerals

Here is a quick rundown of essential vitamins and minerals, so you can see just how important they are.

Vitamin A is essential for healthy growth, skin, teeth and eyes. It helps to maintain both night and colour vision. Vitamin A is found in apricots, pumpkin, peaches, carrots, red and orange peppers, egg yolks and dairy produce.

Vitamin B complex plays a number of roles, including helping the body make energy and promoting blood cells. B vitamins aid digestion and support the immune and nervous systems. Pregnant women are advised to take folic acid (Vitamin B9) supplements to protect their developing babies against neural tube defects. Those of us who suffer low moods probably need more B vitamins in our diet. Eat more beans and alfalfa sprouts, wholegrains, oats, parsley and seaweed. Other sources include meat, green leafy vegetables, dairy produce and egg yolks.

Vitamin C helps cuts and wounds to heal and is good for the immune system, keeping colds at bay. It also helps to prevent heart disease and cancer. The best sources are citrus fruits, kiwi, berries, pomegranate, sweet peppers, cabbage, spinach, broccoli, cauliflower, potatoes and squashes.

Vitamin D helps the body make strong bones and teeth by aiding calcium absorption. It is also good for the muscles and works with Vitamins A and C to boost the immune system. Regular exposure to sunlight is vital to help the body manufacture Vitamin D. Foods that contain reasonable amounts of Vitamin D are tuna, salmon, herrings, sardines, eggs and dairy produce.

Vitamin E helps the heart and skin to stay healthy, and the body make red blood cells. It also aids in the protection of the lungs from damage by air pollutants. Vitamin E is found in vegetable oils, almonds, sunflower seeds, wholegrains such as oatmeal and brown rice, eggs, soya products, avocados and broccoli.

Vitamin K helps the blood to clot and is good for bone health. It is primarily found in green leafy vegetables.

Magnesium is an excellent supplement for the brain, aiding memory and stress management. It is wonderful for boosting the immune system. When a client has been diagnosed with cancer I ask them to start taking this supplement. Citrus and dried fruits, tomatoes, garlic, onions, potatoes, carrots, aubergines (eggplant), nuts and seeds, bread, fish, meat, dairy produce and green vegetables are good sources.

Calcium helps build bones and teeth and maintain a healthy heart. Good sources are dairy produce, sardines, soya products (including tofu/beancurd), almonds and sesame seeds (including hummus).

Sodium helps to regulate the balance of fluid in the body. It aids the contraction and expansion of muscles. Sodium occurs naturally in most foods but our main source is packaged foods and added salt (for good health it is recommended that we should eat no more than 6g salt per day).

Iron is necessary for growth and brain development, and is also used to make haemoglobin, the substance that carries oxygen round the body in the red blood cells. If you don't have enough iron, you can become anaemic. Symptoms include tiredness, lack of concentration and, in severe cases, breathlessness (as your body isn't getting enough oxygen). Most anaemia can be treated by taking an iron supplement, but it is always important to consult your doctor. The best source of iron in food is red meat, liver and egg yolks. Vegetarians can absorb iron from fortified breakfast cereals, dried apricots and figs, oatmeal, spinach, avocados, sunflower and sesame seeds (including hummus).

Selenium is an antioxidant supporting the immune system. It is found in Brazil nuts, shellfish, fresh fruit and vegetables, wheat germ and bran.

Potassium helps muscles and nerves to function and is useful in maintaining a healthy blood pressure. Good sources are mushrooms, bananas and spinach.

Zinc is good for brain function as well as helping the immune and nervous systems. It is contained in fish and shellfish, red meat, poultry, berries, wholegrains, dairy produce, brown rice, nuts and seeds.

Caterpillars don't accept food that's tough or waxy, as it is not nourishing enough. They know that anything that slows down growth is dangerous. You need to eat the best food you can. That doesn't mean expensive food; we can eat well even on a budget so long as the food is fresh and varied.

A healthy lunch could be a rainbow salad of different vegetables. Why absorb vitamins in tablet form when you can enjoy that goodness in fresh fruit and vegetables? Try tuna sandwiches with ripe tomatoes. Sunflower seeds, mixed nuts and raisins make a great mid-afternoon snack. Or choose a piece of fruit over a bar of chocolate to give yourself a healthy energy boost. Try new things. Caterpillars change their feeding patterns according to their nutritional needs.

In the evenings mix vegetables and chicken with plain rice. Add some pineapple and mango. Get creative with herbs and spices. A pot of home-made lentil and vegetable soup is economical and delicious with crusty bread. Pasta accompanied with some fresh tomatoes and mushrooms – *et voilá*! A baked salmon steak sprinkled with pepper and served with sweet potatoes and some broccoli is heaven on a plate! Oily fish is a good source of brain power – eat it two or three times a week. Cook organic lamb and add beans for extra nutrition. Or what about a baked potato covered with cheese? Cheap and nutritious.

Remember that you are growing from a caterpillar into a beautiful butterfly. Make a conscious effort to eat healthily today.

How to eat

It's not just what you eat but *how* you eat that's important. Most people eat too quickly. Eating slowly helps you to enjoy your food and allows you to be alert to the signal that your body is sated. It has been proven that people who eat slowly take in fewer calories and have a greater feeling of fullness. Also, the body is better able to digest and absorb the nutrients from food that is well chewed.

It is important to heed your body's signals. Don't continue eating when your body is saying it's had enough – unless you want to feel bloated. Over time the stomach gradually expands to allow more capacity. A vicious cycle is set in motion. A bigger stomach means you can eat more and more, without feeling full.

Learn from the caterpillar:

- Eat small, frequent meals rather than one large meal a day.

- Take small bites and chew your food well.

- Know your limits – the caterpillar's casing can only stretch so far.

Remember the following too:

- Don't eat after 8.30 pm, as it's harder for food to be digested then.

- Remain upright for 30 minutes after eating so that gravity can aid digestion and don't go to bed with a full stomach.

- Learn to relax. Stress produces stomach acid, resulting in indigestion.

- Drink plenty of water. This is one of the most important things you can do for your body.

Healthy weight

For many people body weight is an issue. Whether we can admit it or not, excess weight usually means that we are repressing emotional issues. We're either choosing unhealthy foods that fail to nourish our bodies or bingeing for comfort. Food becomes a control or coping mechanism. We eat rather than deal with our emotional baggage.

Unless there is a physical problem causing the excess weight, our body is trying to communicate emotional distress. What people see on the outside is a mirror image of how we feel on the inside. We don't comment on other people's weight – it's considered rude. Because of this reluctance to address the issue, people don't get the help they need.

Some of us use food in a different way – by trying not to eat at all. Lack of self-worth spirals into an eating disorder. People who suffer with anorexia nervosa find security in controlling an aspect of their lives – but risk killing themselves. They soothe their soul by punishing their body.

The way you eat is your way of coping with life. If you are severely over- or underweight you are not coping with your emotions. Your body is crying out, but you don't hear it. When you ignore your emotions you are invalidating your pain, saying it's not real. You think you should cope and be stronger than you are. But you are actually making your pain worse by holding it inside. It won't go away. It just gets worse. Repressed pain manifests itself as disease and discomfort.

When you believe in yourself, you mirror that image to the world. What does *your* image say to the world?

Weight is a huge issue – enough for a book on its own. To be healthy and live a good life, we have to be aware of our body and listen to what it says. Just by eating nutritious food and taking regular exercise you can start to lead a healthy life. Don't waste money on diets that don't work. When you start to eat in the old way again, the weight goes right back on. If you have a tendency to over-eat, work out what your triggers are. Use a food diary to see how your emotions are causing you to seek comfort in food, and which foods you have a history of over-eating.

Too many people try to heal on their own. I want to stress here the importance of finding support and encouragement. You need to surround yourself with people who understand and don't judge. When we open our hearts to the universe and become willing to change, we are halfway to healing. Just be open to new ideas.

Insomnia

Poor dietary habits are one way that we rob ourselves of energy. Disturbed sleep is another. The amount of sleep we require depends on our age. Most children need 12 hours. Deepak Chopra tells us that children sleep so well because they have no worries or anxieties. Their minds are free from stress. Adults function best on around seven or eight hours, but a huge percentage of the population survives on far less. Our sleep is disturbed by negative thinking. We sabotage our sleep reserves, depriving ourselves of rest, torturing ourselves with "what if?" and "why not?".

Insomniacs usually suffer "racing" minds – a Formula One race track inside their heads. In this state, the brain is simply unable to shut down and heal itself. Sleeplessness has terrible consequences – at work, in our relationships and on our finances. Motorists can fall asleep at the wheel due to overwork and stress – instead of taking "me time" and learning to relax, they are literally driving on "empty" and can cause terrible accidents.

People who suffer major trauma can go into a coma – deep sleep. This is the body's way of healing itself. Sleep is the great restorer. So if you have problems sleeping, this is where you can help yourself. And I'm not talking about pills. No one should have to be on long-term medication for insomnia. And that's not just my opinion. The neurologist Marc Raphaelson, for example, has commented that insomnia is traditionally seen as a symptom of an underlying condition, and that any drugs used to counter insomnia should be approved only for the short term, until the primary condition can be treated. He also stresses that 85 percent of insomnia sufferers can be treated, using a combination of behavioural therapy and medicine.

I can understand why people pop pills – desperation. Our bodies need sleep. Deprived of sleep one day, the body requires more the next. But we need to start *educating* people instead of giving them drugs. Insomnia can be greatly helped, even eliminated, by changing the way we think.

Using your self-relaxation techniques (see pages 30–32) will be the start of changing your sleep patterns. Just think how good you will feel awakening in the morning refreshed, re-energized and fully wide awake, ready for the day ahead. When did you last feel like that? Isn't it time to start?

Your commitment to change is the start of a whole new life. You will sleep better, feel better and look better. You'll feel more in control of your life. Do you want to know my Butterfly Experience Prescription for Health?:

It is VITAL that you think POSITIVE THOUGHTS.

It is VITAL that you use POSITIVE WORDS.

It is VITAL that you ACT POSITIVELY.

Using positive language and your Butterfly Experience Affirmations on a daily basis, you will really start to feel the benefit. It's as good as medicine. Your thoughts should always be positive; your words to yourself and others should be kind and loving. You should act positively all the time, creating a good behaviour pattern. All this contributes to a healthy body.

The Butterfly Experience Health Plan

By following the Butterfly Experience Health Plan you are taking the first important steps to creating a new healthy you. Caterpillars have weak sight – I want to help you see how vital your health is to your new life. The steps to health below are crucial. Start the Butterfly Experience Health Plan today and feel the difference.

1. If you are worried or anxious about any part of your body, please consult your doctor for advice.

2. Make sure your doctor refers you to a consultant or specialist, if appropriate.

3. Find out as much as you can about your condition and the various treatments that are available. Your body already knows how to heal itself. As soon as treatment starts, it will go into action to heal itself naturally.

4. Consider changing your diet and your lifestyle.

5. Realize that having a positive mindset will help you to heal more quickly. *You Can Heal Your Life* by Louise L. Hay is an excellent book that will help you continue the process of clearing out your negative thinking and help you to start loving yourself more.

6. Use the Butterfly Experience self-relaxation techniques (see pages 30–32). I know no more powerful treatment.

7. Have an open mind. Be willing to change if necessary. Look to the future in a positive way. It is time for you

to accept and heal. Few people are aware of how their *thought life* has impacted on them physically. How is your thinking affecting your health?

8. Remember that you are treating the mind, body and spirit, helping each aspect to feel healthier.

9. Accept help.

10. Stop only pleasing others. Make yourself number one.

Metamorphosis

At the end of its life stage, the caterpillar seeks out a safe place to evolve again, entering into the third stage of its metamorphosis. The series of instars lies behind. Now the caterpillar constructs a leaf shelter for protection and, using a silken girdle, it attaches itself safely to its chosen place, encased in a chrysalis. The chrysalis turns a beautiful bronze or golden colour, as if in celebration of the wonders that are about to take place … Can you feel it happening?

You think this is good? Wait till the next stage!

STAGE THREE · THE COCOON

Going Within

CHAPTER THIRTEEN

———————

The Cocoon

THE COCOON STAGE IS where the miracle happens – it's a mysterious, fascinating facet of the Butterfly Experience. In it you stop your wanderings and rest in your quest – to take stock. You look to the future, to the "reveal", where you emerge as the miracle you're supposed to be. In the Cocoon stage you go within. You strengthen and prepare yourself for the final stage of your transformation. This is where you change from being a bizarre, ugly, defensive caterpillar and become your authentic Self.

Far from being a dormant stage, within the cocoon (chrysalis) an amazing metamorphosis is taking place. Each stage creates fabulous patterns and colours that will differentiate us from others. And there is inner movement. A butterfly's wings have to be strong before it can fly. Inside the cocoon it makes tiny movements, building up its strength. If the cocoon were to split prematurely, the butterfly would die, so be very kind to yourself at this time.

Let's recap. In the first stage of the Butterfly Experience you came to know yourself better. You learned to recognize what is holding you back. The second stage helped you to identify and remove those blocks to progress. It gave you an energy boost for the important work ahead. The Cocoon stage takes these ideas a step farther and asks you to go *even deeper* within, posing the important questions that heal, so you can go on to live a magnificent life. Here you will build on and develop the seven vital qualities that maximize the Butterfly Experience:

DESIRE

SELF-BELIEF

PERSEVERANCE

TRUST

DETERMINATION

SELF-DISCIPLINE

GRATITUDE

As you read the next section, ask yourself if you have these qualities in good measure. Be honest – what do you still have to work on? Which areas still need fortifying?

Desire

*What things soever ye desire, when ye pray, believe
that ye receive them, and ye shall have them.*

THE BIBLE, MARK 11:24

Sir Richard Branson is a maverick who has transformed the
way business operates in the UK. He left school at 16, having
struggled with dyslexia. Nowadays it would be easy to feel
that qualifications are a must-have to get on in life. But what
if you don't have those exam results in your pocket? If *that's*
been your excuse up till now, it's time to think again. Did you
know that many top business people don't have degrees? At
the age of 18 Branson founded Virgin Records. By the age
of 24 he had bought one of the Virgin Islands. Yet despite
being a multi-millionaire, Richard still has a burning *desire*
to be successful. He never takes success for granted. And he
still has fire in his belly. He rewards his staff with handsome
bonuses as a thank you for their hard work. And far from
kicking back and enjoying the good life, he's an advocate for
the environment. Virgin, one of his companies, follows the
Gaia Capitalism approach and is concerned about the health
of our planet. The world has to be saved if we want to continue evolving.

Let me give you another example. Back at the beginning
of the last century, Henry Ford was a man with no qualifications from an extremely poor background. His desire
was to create a horseless carriage. Ford, like Branson, was
prepared to do things differently, changing the way cars
were manufactured. He paid his staff high wages and had

a global vision for the wealth he created. Most of his fortune was left to the Ford Foundation, which still encourages
education around the world.

We all have a deep burning desire for success. We all
need and want to be recognized for our contribution, for
our unique talents. Not everyone's talents are best suited to
the world of business. Sometimes it's hard to admit even to
ourselves that we don't want to follow a conventional path.
There's a lot of pressure from parents, teachers and friends
to take the established route to "success". But is your path
right for you?

Ask yourself, "What do I truly consider success to be?" If
we're on a path that's wrong for us, success may feel hollow.
Happiness does not always come from what others would
have hoped for us. For me, success means simply being the
best you can be.

JOURNAL: EXERCISE NINE

What Is Success?

- Turn to your Butterfly Experience Journal and write
  down what you consider success to be. List all the
  things that you think make people successful and also
  write down what would make *you* feel successful. Trust
  your instinct. Don't judge or edit yourself in the process.
  Some word or phrase will jump out at you and give you
  another piece of your jigsaw. When you find it, there will
  be an inner knowing. Excitement.

- Also write down the three actions you need to take to improve your success.

My own desire has always been to help others. Over the years it became so strong that, after qualifying in clinical hypnosis, I decided to invest my own money in opening a clinic. I started out as a single practitioner while still managing to run a home, look after three children and further my training in the evenings. Without a burning desire to make a success of my new business I might have given up. Desire is the best motivator I know – the hard work soon began to pay off. Before long I had built myself up as an expert in my field and was enjoying an excellent reputation.

Desire starts inside us – that's where the magic is. It's always there, buoying us up and telling us to keep going when things backfire. Desire insists that we find alternatives and reminds us that setbacks just make us stronger. Desire is what fuels our perseverance; it's the fire in our bellies that makes us go on. Mother Teresa's desire was to help the sick, the orphaned and the dying, and she became one of the best-loved human beings the world has ever known.

> *Yesterday is gone. Tomorrow has not yet come.*
> *We have only today. Let us begin.*
>
> **MOTHER TERESA (1910–1997)**

Whenever I read autobiographies of people I admire, I get a sense of their desire. The British boxer Frank Bruno wanted to be World Heavyweight Champion. His book describes how he was beaten on three attempts until he learned his lesson – that he had to work harder. Frank's desire to become world champion was so powerful, it was "like a drug". That's a great analogy – and that's how badly you have to want it. Your desire has to be strong enough to keep you going when times are hard.

On his fourth attempt Frank's desire paid off. He became World Champion. He never gave up, and kept his focus and vision. What do you want out of your life? The desire to succeed requires a certain quality – it has to be 100 percent. When you truly *believe* that you can achieve your desire, things automatically begin to happen. I never, ever give up. Which is not to say that I've not met difficulties along the way. But my desire to succeed can withstand any knocks. I never use the word "failure". I don't believe in it. I believe in learning from my mistakes. I believe in using desire to push past boundaries and take me out of my comfort zone to a place where I can achieve success. And you can do it too.

To achieve your true desires you must first make them real. And then you have to invest energy in them.

> *Success usually comes to those who are too*
> *busy to be looking for it.*
> **HENRY DAVID THOREAU (1817–1862)**

A word of warning: many people have achieved financial success, only to find that their business crashes and they lose everything, including home, marriage and friendships. Their desire to achieve made them successful, but they lost focus on what was really important in life. Not material things, but values and standards.

Self-belief

Billy Connelly, the Scottish comedian, said that he knew he was going to be a comedian at the age of six. "You get what you'll believe you'll get," he said. "You have to really want it and you'll get it."

Our DNA, like our fingerprint, identifies each of us as a unique individual. I believe our *self-belief* does that too. Self-belief is imperative. With it we can overcome any challenge. We must absolutely rid our minds of negative thoughts. If we don't believe in ourselves then how can we expect others to believe in us? When we have self-belief we give off a positive energy. We approach tasks in a more positive way. And our attitude is contagious.

How often have you heard movie stars or musicians say they just *knew* that it was going to happen for them. They believed it so much that they actually created their own opportunities. Regardless of the opinions of others, they believed anything was possible. Believing in ourselves starts in our hearts. That's where the magic is.

I received an email from Rose, an Australian who had moved to Rome. Rose is a fashion designer and always had the dream of selling her own designer collection in Italy. While browsing in a bookstore, Rose came across a book called *L'Esperienza della Farfalla*. She was intrigued as the title of the book encapsulated exactly how she wanted to express her own collection of designs. The book was *The Butterfly Experience*, which had been translated into Italian. She had been searching for something that would tell her she was on the right path of her dream.

When she found the book, she knew that her thoughts and ideas would become a reality. After reading a few chapters she felt the urge to let me know that the book was giving her the security and courage to face the obstacles that she had to overcome. Her dream was to hold a fashion show of her own collection at an event in Rome and leave the audience feeling positive, uplifted and inspired.

I gave Rose the encouragement and inspiration to never give up on her dream. It wasn't long before she contacted me to say that she had met someone who had offered her the opportunity to stage a fashion show. This would give her the experience she needed to hold her own event with her own collection later in the year. She was so grateful that she had trusted in herself and in the Butterfly Experience.

The American track athlete Gail Devers, who won three Olympic gold medals during her career, wrote that you must "Keep your dreams alive. Understand to achieve anything requires faith and belief in yourself, vision, hard work, determination and dedication. Remember all things are possible for those who believe."

Do you believe in yourself? Do you truly believe that you can achieve what you set out to accomplish? If the answer to those questions wasn't a resounding "Yes!", don't give up hope. All beliefs are learned beliefs. Our self-belief is shaped in the cradle of our family and our environment. Sometimes children are conditioned to believe that they're not as good as their siblings or their friends. This is simply not true. We are all different and we all have unique gifts. Any negative beliefs that you have about yourself can be altered. This process is already underway within you. The

Egg and Caterpillar stages have identified the old beliefs that were harming you. Now you have to be clear what your *new* beliefs are.

To do this you will need to use the visualization technique in Chapter 15 (see pages 168–9). Using it, you'll learn to eradicate old, damaging ideas, see the best in yourself, and imagine enjoying what you really want. When you really believe that good things are possible – a pay rise, a better relationship with your boss, greater opportunities to show what you can do – your behaviour starts to change. Your attitude changes. You look and sound more confident. Confidence is a by-product of increased self-belief. Like setting off a chain reaction, visualization can bring about the changes you want.

Harrison Ford said this about success: "You've got to find it on your own terms – don't imitate others." When you start to believe in *who* you are, not *what* you are, life becomes abundant – and that abundance comes in many guises. A strong *desire* and real *self-belief* – these factors alone can help people achieve the impossible.

When we act badly or think negatively, we subconsciously transmit that to others. Gossiping, backstabbing, laziness – none of these have any place in a positive life. When you feel good about yourself you radiate positive energy, and that makes you attractive to others. Remember, we can't afford to compromise on who we are. Be yourself.

I have always believed in myself. Through my own desire, self-belief, perseverance, trust, determination, self-discipline and gratitude, this book was written. I never gave up on my dream of sharing my vision, of helping to change the vibration of the world. And I always knew this book would be a best-seller!

Except ye see signs and wonders, ye will not believe.

THE BIBLE, JOHN 4:48

Perseverance

Combine *perseverance* with the other ingredients for success, and life gives us rewards. I believe that each and every one of us has the determination to achieve. We just need the right motivation and then we have to dig deep.

There are so many positive examples of this quality in history. One of my favourite quotes is from Sir Winston Churchill (1874–1965): *"Never give in – never, never, never, never ...."* And Churchill led a nation to victory!

We don't have to look far for other amazing stories of perseverance. Nelson Mandela was imprisoned for 27 years in South Africa. Determined to survive to tell the world about his country's story, he kept himself motivated by using positive statements every day. He never stopped believing that he would see his country free of apartheid. Even from his prison cell he worked ceaselessly toward his goal.

How badly do you want your dream? How determined are you to achieve success? Perseverance makes you pick yourself up when you're down. There are times when I feel below par, but I know that no one can pick me up but myself.

I always seem to find an inner strength and the determination to go on ... because I go looking for it!

We don't get good at anything unless we practise. That's exactly what you have to do with the Butterfly Experience techniques. Remember that you brought years of negative thinking to this experience. Similarly, we can't expect the people around us to change overnight. Change has to start with us.

Nothing in the world can take the place of persistence.

CALVIN COOLIDGE (1872–1933)

You're learning how to become a new you, with new thoughts and new ideas. You don't need to wait until you get to the end of the book before making changes. You can decide right here, right now that this is the beginning of something wonderful. If something feels right, have the courage to do what's needed. With NO restrictions. Change is scary, but so is staying stagnant. Don't deprive yourself.

Walt Disney was sitting with his two daughters in a local park, with very little to amuse them, when he had a vision. In it he saw people from all over the world – children and adults alike – having the time of their lives in a wonderful theme park. As he sat thinking about his dream, he began to wonder how he could achieve his goal. Where could the park be? What would it cost? How could he convince banks to fund it?

We all have ideas. We all daydream. What made Disney different? *He never gave up.* Even after being turned down by banks 302 times for funding for his project, he kept on going. It took years of hard work, raising finance and dealing with disappointments, but Disney stayed focused on his goal. Some 10 years on, by 1965, 50 million people had gone through the gates of Disneyland.

Like Disney we need a feeling of adventure when we set out our goals, a fantasy in our head. We need frontier spirit as we head for our "Tomorrowland". Too many people nowadays want everything handed to them without working for it. How about you? If you don't get that promotion, will you walk away? If a business fails, are you prepared to start all over again? Are you prepared to learn from your experience?

Perseverance will get you what you want. It's said that 90 percent of people in life are less successful than they should be because they fall at the first hurdle. It is only the "stubborn" 10 percent with grit who learn the lessons they need to. Those lessons make them stronger and better prepared for the next time. Never stop believing that your success is just around the corner!

We haven't failed. We now know a thousand things that won't work, so we're that much closer to finding what will.

THOMAS ALVA EDISON (1847–1931)

Trust

"Trust" is a very small word, but has a huge impact on our lives. If we cannot *trust* ourselves then how can we expect anyone else to trust us? We trust the medical profession when we need their help. We put our lives in their hands and trust that all will be well. We trust our friends, colleagues and family. We know that they'll be there for us in times of need. Trust is a very powerful, very intimate act.

Now we have to build on our belief in ourselves and trust Spirit. This is extremely hard – we fear the loss of control. We have to work on trust each and every day for the rest of our lives. But it's the answer to our fears. Without trust in a Greater Reality we are totally reliant on ourselves. And we know how easily we make mistakes. God is our Provider. When we put our trust in Spirit to the test, especially when life is at its most painful, we trust that He will see us through. In the Bible, St Peter's trust wavered when Jesus stretched out his hand to him and commanded that he walk across the angry waters. Jesus was asking for his trust. This story tells us that we need to trust in God absolutely. We have to believe God will supply whatever it is that we need. We only have to ask. For years I sought proof – but I've learned over the years that trusting brings miracles. And you can't explain them – otherwise they wouldn't be miracles.

Having thus chosen our course, without guile and with pure purpose, let us renew our trust in God, and go forward without fear and with manly hearts.

ABRAHAM LINCOLN (1809–1865)

Trust is a vital ingredient in a happy life. It is vital in others – we should surround ourselves only with people with whom we feel instinctively secure. And above all, *we* have to be trustworthy. We have to follow through on our promises if we are to find the sort of friendship that truly sustains us. Being a trustworthy person, acting honourably, living according to spiritual principles at all times – these things also change how we feel about ourselves. Learning to trust takes courage.

Even if you've been hurt in the past, don't allow past events to stop you experiencing happiness today. It doesn't have to be a revolutionary change in character, an overnight thing. Remember the cocoon and all those tiny movements that one day will bring release.

> *Men of genius are admired, men of wealth*
> *are envied, men of power are feared; but only*
> *men of character are trusted.*
>
> **ALFRED ADLER (1870–1937)**

Determination

Life coach Anthony Robbins said: "Determination is the wake-up call to the human will." The American inventor Thomas Alva Edison (1847–1931) is an example of a man who became successful because he mastered the art of *determination*. He tried over five thousand times before he was able to make the first working light bulb. Every time an experiment failed he looked to see what he could learn from it. It would have been tempting to give up after the first thousand or two thousand times, don't you think? But winners never quit, and quitters never win. I *never* take "No" for an answer. No matter what the task, I will always find a way to make it work and I'll keep going until it does. It's in my blood, my DNA.

You only get back in life what you give out. If I keep on striving to be the best, someone or something turns up to help me. It's that trust thing again. You have to believe it will happen. Here in Scotland Sir Tom Hunter made his mark and his fortune in commerce. Tom is someone I greatly admire for his determination. He has been knighted for his vision as an entrepreneur and for his philanthropy. Did you know that Tom began his career selling sports shoes out of the back of a van? Life hasn't always been easy for him, even after he made his fortune.

Tom's motivation has always been to help educate young adults and he has given away millions in donations to children's causes. One of the wealthiest people in the world today, Tom understands the need to pass on what he has been given. His Hunter Foundation is inspirational. But Tom's attitude of *never give up* inspires me more.

Determination builds character. It makes us better people. It helps us to prioritize and maximize our time for positive results. Determination is a tool – it lets us win in spite of our limitations. Determination gets us out of trouble. Determination is what helps us to improve our relationships and achieve great things.

Self-discipline

Norman Vincent Peale (1898–1993), author of *The Power of Positive Thinking*, said: "If you put off everything till you're sure of it, you'll never get anything done."

Lack of *self-discipline* is a common source of low self-esteem. How many times have you said to yourself, "I wish I had more will power!"? How many times have you started to do something, only to give up at the first hurdle? We've all had experiences like these. Say you want to stop smoking. You start the day telling yourself you're going to stop. But by lunchtime you are having a cigarette. Why? You need more self-discipline.

If only people could learn to trust in their energy sources and be stronger in order to stop smoking. The nicotine addiction is the problem, not the cigarettes. When you start smoking your body gets hooked on the nicotine – a substance that causes poor health and disease. Smoking is proven to kill, so I urge you now, if you are thinking about stopping, then this is the time to think self-discipline and STOP TODAY. By learning to use the Red-X and self-relaxation techniques, and drinking plenty of water to purify your system, you can make great shifts in your energy and nicotine addiction.

What *is* self-discipline? Self-discipline is doing what needs to be done, regardless of how you're feeling. Self-discipline shreds problems. It stops us procrastinating, it makes our lives more orderly, it allows us to solve problems *today*. Combined with the goal-setting ideas I'm going to teach you later in the book (see pages 191–8), self-discipline is a powerful tool.

People make the mistake of thinking that just because they fail to follow through on something big, they should give up entirely. Self-discipline is like spiritual muscle – the more you use it, the stronger it becomes. The paradox is that it takes self-discipline to become more self-disciplined. So set yourself targets – small goals at first – and follow through on them. Make a new business contact. Create or review your Facebook page. Make the phone call that you've been putting off. Every day set yourself simple tasks, and at the end of the day tick them off in your journal.

Gradually increase the challenge. Telling someone you trust what you're doing will help – they can hold you accountable. Every day, up the ante. Enjoy the benefits of a life of self-discipline and soon there will be no going back. Every time you succeed at something give yourself a small reward. Self-discipline is a vital characteristic of success because it helps us to control our reactions. Now that you know how to temper your negative emotions and learn lessons from every situation, developing self-discipline is going to be so much easier. Affirm your new self-discipline to yourself daily.

We all have dreams. But in order to make dreams come into reality, it takes an awful lot of determination, self-discipline and effort.

JESSE OWENS (1913–1980)

Gratitude

Do you sometimes think you're the only one the rain falls on? Catch yourself wondering what you did to deserve X, Y and Z? It's draining and time-wasting. Use some of the self-discipline we were just talking about to start thinking in a more positive manner. When you find yourself thinking negatively, ask yourself: "What have I *learned* from this experience? How could I have done things differently?" Acknowledge the feelings and emotions that you become aware of. Then move on, using the self-relaxation technique. Visualize the way you would have liked the situation to be and write down your thoughts. The next time a similar situation arises, act on them.

Now let's look at what gratitude really means. It means being grateful for *all* the things in your life.

JOURNAL: EXERCISE TEN

Gratitude

Turn to your Butterfly Experience Journal and look over your gratitude list from Exercise Four.

- Now I want you to add three more non-materialistic things that you are grateful for.

Really consider what you are grateful for. If you're struggling, think about the starving of the world. No running water, no food, no shelter. How do you feel about your life now? You don't have to spend money to feel blessed. Gratitude is about your attitude to life. One man might sit in front of the TV, beer in hand, moaning about the state of the world. Another might sit in the same room enjoying the programme that others have made for him and the company of his precious family. Life is precious. And it can be short. It's so easy to forget that, until something happens.

Let us rise up and be thankful, for if we didn't learn a lot today, at least we learned a little, and if we didn't learn a little, at least we didn't get sick, and if we got sick, at least we didn't die; so, let us all be thankful.

THE BUDDHA (*c.* 563–*c.* 483 BCE)

Your self-image

All these character traits stem from a key concept that we have to address in the Cocoon stage.

As you've worked through this book, you've learned to be calmer, to focus your attention on what you want. Now it's time for one of the most important challenges that the Butterfly Experience offers – changing your relationship with YOU. If I asked you what is the most important relationship in your life, most of you would probably name your partner, your children or your parents. I'm asking you to consider another idea: that the most important relationship you will ever have in life is with *yourself.*

Self-image is vital for good self-esteem. It affects personality, moulds behaviour and colours attitude. If it's good, it helps confidence. If it's poor, people are able to tell immediately. What we think about ourselves shapes who we are.

How is your self-image? Do you wake up in the morning feeling fantastic? Do you feel good about yourself on the inside? Do you believe that you are a fabulous, happy, healthy, sexy, gorgeous, loving, caring, compassionate, special human being? Or do those words make you cringe? Ask yourself why you find it so difficult to accept the way you are. Ask yourself that question, then listen to the answer you receive. Listen to what your body is telling you – the more you baulk at positive statements about yourself, the more you need to do this work! Do you put yourself down? Do you let others put you down? Without self-esteem our mood is dependent on the good graces of others – because we haven't learned to be happy in our own skin.

As Phil MacGraw, the American psychologist and host of the television show *Dr Phil* puts it, "You have the power to be miserable the rest of your life. Or you can say, 'I'm going to give myself the permission to heal.'" He stresses that it's up to you to choose what sort of relationship you have with yourself and remove the obstacles that are blocking your way to living the best life you can.

Without a positive self-image, it's impossible to have a full, loving relationship with anyone else. Negative thoughts about ourselves inevitably impact on those around us. Problems creep in, often repeating themselves time and time again – because we haven't yet learned our lessons. Do you constantly try to please? Are you trying to be what you think others want you to be? Are you living your life to please your parents? Do you get jittery every time you have to say no?

We learn from our elders, of course. Their insecurities influence the way they rear or mentor us. We sometimes grow up believing that we're not good enough. Acknowledging that helps. But sometimes we get stuck in a rut of blaming others, rather than moving on. Is that true of you? Is there resentment in your life that's holding you back? How long are you prepared to blame the past for the way your life is today?

Yes, we were conditioned as children, but every new day is a chance to refocus, rethink, recharge. You're an adult now – you choose the direction your life takes. A new relationship with yourself is the true start of your new life. It's important that you understand this. Every relationship we have moves to a new level as soon as we drop the idea that we can find happiness in another person. All relationships stem from our sense of self. Friendships blossom as you come to love and appreciate yourself. Romance deepens because you're willing your partner to grow with you. Love for your children becomes a free channel, no longer blocked by false expectations.

So, what kind of relationship do you have with your mind? With your body? With your spirit? Are you frightened to find out? What if I told you that everyone else knows how you feel about yourself just by *looking* at you! When we have low self-esteem it shows. A lack of confidence means that we hold our body in a certain manner – shoulders rounded and defensive body language. It shows in the way we dress. It shows in our use of eye contact, or lack of it. Inability to meet someone's gaze means that we are experiencing emotional pain. I'm going to work with you now on a technique to help you address that pain.

CHAPTER FOURTEEN

Mirror Work

Reflections from the inside out

THE COCOON STAGE IS AMAZING. It allows the caterpillar to completely disassemble. The transformation of a caterpillar into a butterfly is one of the wonders of the world. A mystery beyond description. No one knows exactly how every cell moves to a predetermined place to reassemble the caterpillar into the shape of a butterfly – a new form, capable of flight.

Mirror work allows you to see the wonder of your metamorphosis. It helps you to face up to the truth about yourself, and it magically transforms you. And isn't that what the Cocoon stage is all about?

There are two types of mirror work. First of all, let's talk about your body. Do you like every part of it? Do you like your face, even when you are tired and look a little puffy in the morning? You have to appreciate your body even when you're not well or your energy is low. You have to learn to love yourself, no matter what you look like.

What's stopping you from feeling good about yourself and accepting yourself exactly the way you are? Why do you keep comparing yourself to others? We see pictures every day of famous women with anorexia nervosa or bulimia – tortured souls trying to live up to the false ideal of what the fashion world considers beautiful. The media bombards us with images of skeletal young women that we're supposed to think are the norm. People go to extreme lengths to achieve those idealized images: false breasts, hair extensions, liposuction, collagen lips, cheek enhancements … Where will it end? And what are the long-term effects? No one undergoes surgery like that unless they have a fundamental problem with body image. Look at the terrible results in some unfortunates – misshapen features, tumerous lips. Why take the risk?

It's not just women who sabotage their bodies. Men are competing with airbrushed photographs of genetically blessed youths who have a team of people working to keep them in optimum health. They pump their bodies with steroids and use weights until they're bulging with muscles. They have become addicted to the idea of the perfect body shape. When will the world wake up to that fact that we're all individuals? When will we start accepting our diversity and loving who we are, not how we look? Your genetic composition is yours alone. *Be proud of that.* It's time to celebrate your uniqueness.

When was the last time you looked at yourself naked? Really looked, not just long enough to pull a face at what you don't like.

Take a good look at yourself in the mirror today. What do you see?

We are all spirit beings in a physical body. Ask your body how it feels today. Can you feel self-doubt? Uncertainty? Keep working through it, moving around your body in your thoughts – I guarantee that this technique will very quickly teach you to move forward in a gentle and loving way. Beauty on the outside is linked with the beauty that lies deep inside us. It is a reflection of a happy spirit. What we wear on the outside is a reflection of how we feel about ourselves inside. Do you feel good enough about yourself to take care of yourself? Do you exercise in a way that you enjoy? Are you nourishing yourself properly?

Do you try to cover up your body with baggy, ill-fitting clothes, or do you hide behind the latest trends? So many people think that if they buy new clothes, they will feel better. Yes, that's true … for all of five minutes. But if you don't feel good on the inside, no amount of clothes will change the way you feel.

Do you take joy in your appearance or could you not care less how you look? When I look in the mirror I see a gorgeous, wonderful, caring, compassionate woman. I truly love myself for who I am and what I stand for. Can you say that about yourself?

We cannot buy happiness, nor make it. Happiness comes from within.

Love it or hate it, your body is with you for life unless you undergo plastic surgery, and even then you are only changing the outside. You are still you on the inside. Your body will carry you on your journey no matter where you go. Take a few moments to just think about how much your body has endured so far.

Look at yourself in the mirror again. Decide to thank your body every day for the hard work it does. It has never given up on you, no matter how hard you've punished it. Look at your body as the body of someone who deserves to be happy, who deserves to lead an abundant life. Your body needs to be looked after, cared for. It needs exercise to keep it healthy. Do you allow the sun to burn your skin? Do you ever think about that fresh, pure skin that needs moisturizer to maintain its softness?

Do you take a brisk walk every day or do you sit in front of the TV and moan about celebrities who are stick thin? This is your body and only you can think yourself healthy and slim. Once you think the thoughts, the physical changes will happen. You become who you think you are. Make a commitment today to nurture and care for yourself. You would do it for a child, so why not for yourself? Most people think that you no longer need to look after your body when you reach adulthood. For as long as you are on this Earth you must take care of yourself. You are the most special thing. You have Life itself and it is precious. Nurture and care for yourself and your body will take you a long way. I believe that by looking after yourself properly, you can extend the length of your life.

JOURNAL: EXERCISE ELEVEN
Mirror Work

Turn to your Butterfly Experience Journal for your mirror work exercise.

- Have a good look at yourself in a mirror. Write down all the good things you notice about your appearance – your warm smile, for example.

- Now write down the three things you need to do to improve your image. These could be as easy as applying some make-up or having a haircut.

Looking at the inside

To help you keep making good decisions about your body, let's look inside you. It's time for the next stage of mirror work – for one of the most powerful techniques I know.

So many of us feel angry with ourselves. Deep down we *know* we've been complicit in things that have gone wrong. We're angry at ourselves for not standing up for what was right. Angry that we didn't do or say what was needed. We've allowed hundreds of tiny grievances to pile up until they became a great weight that threatens us.

We resent others, but most of all we resent ourselves. Removing that "resentment of self" is an inside job that takes time. We have to deconstruct the walls we've built to protect our ego. But that's OK. There's no need to rush. This feeling has taken a lifetime to build up. It would be unrealistic to expect it to disappear quickly. But close mirror work will help to get you there.

It would be irresponsible of me not to include a warning here: mirror work is extremely powerful. What you see in the mirror is actually a reflection of your inner self. The *real* you. Some people initially find the experience unsettling or even disturbing. But mirror work helps us to find out who we really are. Through it we overcome anger and resentment. We come to love ourselves. When you look in the mirror – deeply, not superficially – the way you feel about your Self changes. Why? Because by looking at yourself, *really* looking at yourself in the mirror, you start to see your inner child. You come to know that little boy or girl who is still there, deep inside you, and who needs nurturing. Recognizing this, you immediately understand the importance of taking care of the child within. This feeling never goes away. Would you be unkind to your own daughter or son? Then why be unkind to your own inner child?

The kindest thing you can do for your inner child is release the emotions weighing him or her down. We have to free ourselves in order to move on. Let's get started.

Close Mirror Work

This Butterfly Experience exercise requires forethought. You also need space and time – uninterrupted time. Switch off the phone. Sit quietly and comfortably.

1. When you are ready, look into a hand mirror. Ask yourself:

- Who do you see?
- How do you feel?
- Do you feel silly?
- Do you feel embarrassed?
- Do you think, "This won't work"?

All these thoughts will be going around your head. That's perfectly natural. Look again.

2. Look. I mean really *look*. Deep into your eyes. See that little girl or boy. Watch them looking back at you. That little girl or boy inside you, asking you not to hurt yourself anymore. Look into their eyes. What do you want to say to them? And what are they trying to say to you? Sometimes tears come up. That's perfectly acceptable. The tears show that you are feeling vulnerable. You are human and have feelings. Sometimes we've told ourselves so often we're strong that it hurts to see the tired, frightened child who is looking back at us.

3. Look at yourself again and say three positive Butterfly Experience Affirmations to your inner child. You decide what positive statements your inner child needs. For example:

I am healthy, strong and loving.

I am fabulous, confident and wise.

I am happy, loving and kind.

4. Now for the next stage. I want you to close your eyes and imagine the person you want to be. Be specific.

Go into great detail as you fantasize about that person. Ask yourself:

- How would I feel if I were that person?
- What would I look like?
- What would I dress like?
- What would my behaviour tell others?
- What would my career be?
- What would others say about me?
- How would the IDEAL ME feel and look?

5. Open your eyes. Look in the mirror again. Repeat your three affirmations.

NOW HOW DO YOU FEEL?

This exercise is vital in changing your thought patterns to a positive mindset. Practise it every day for 15 minutes. Do this for 30 days. Give yourself a tick in your Butterfly Experience Journal or on your calendar each day. Give yourself a smiley face. If you forget to practise your mirror work, go back to the start of 30 days. You will soon train your mind to remember.

By repeating your positive affirmations every day you'll be reinforcing a positive mindset and boosting your self-esteem. Your attitude to yourself will change. You will feel more vibrant and uplifted. Within *days* your friends will start to see a difference.

Below I have listed examples of positive Butterfly Experience Affirmations suitable for close mirror work. You can choose some of them. But why not make up your own?

I love myself exactly as I am.

I am strong, healthy and confident.

I am open to change.

My body radiates love.

Change is just another challenge.

I deserve the best, nothing but the best.

I attract all the abundance in the world.

I give of myself to others.

We owe it to ourselves to treat ourselves with respect, kindness, dignity and love. Every day we grow another day older. Don't waste your time on Earth. Every day when you wake up, tell your inner child how happy and loved he or she is. Constantly reinforce your new self-belief. Things don't have to be perfect, so long as you are moving forward. How quickly do you want change to happen? Tick off those days as you practise Close Mirror Work, and see the difference!

Setting boundaries

Now that you are using mirror work to come face to face with the inner you, it's time to think about your boundaries. This section is about something many people struggle with, but it's a vital life skill. Cocoon with this issue now. Think very deeply about how it affects you. Of all the life areas where the Butterfly Experience can be sabotaged, this is one of the most vulnerable.

The whole purpose of setting up boundaries is to take care of yourself. By doing this you are giving out a signal, stating what you will and will not accept in your life. Unless you let others know how you feel, no one will know – you don't have a glass head. You must learn to speak your truth and be honest – first and foremost with yourself. Often we don't know fully what we want, so it's easier to think about what we don't want when we try to establish boundaries. Stop thinking about how you think others want you to be. Don't give away your power to anyone. Trust your own inner feelings and use your new-found intuition to be who you are. Accept nothing less.

For many years I found it hard to say "No". People pick up on this energy and take advantage. Why do we allow others to do this? Simply because we want them to love us. When I truly learned to love myself, I no longer needed to please others. I set my boundaries and decided that I would be the best that I could be, regardless of others' expectations. This is my life and I am living it with joy and love every day. I know why I am here on Earth and I am fulfilling my vocation. When I approve of myself, I don't need the approval of others. The only way I can approve of myself is to live a life of integrity and be true to myself and the power that is my Source.

I spent time working on my own inner child. This was my healing process. When we start loving ourselves everything changes. Each and every human being has the right to speak their truth. Each person has the right to be treated with dignity and respect. If you respect yourself, then others will respect you. Be assertive and state what you want and need.

This is especially relevant in relationships. Many women allow men to abuse them, mentally, emotionally and physically. Setting your personal boundaries means drawing a line between what you will and will not accept.

You also have to recognize when someone has crossed a boundary. You must be prepared to speak your truth. Otherwise others will keep on pushing you. We learn behaviour – and it can be relearned. It is an attitude and attitudes can be changed. I want you to set your particular Boundary Statement today (see opposite).

Forgiveness

This is great work. But perhaps there's something else you need to do. Perhaps you need a little more encouragement, a little time to focus on ... the power of forgiving.

Are you finally ready to forgive? This decision to act is probably one of the hardest you will have to take. Truly forgiving someone who has hurt you is not easy – and forgiveness isn't just something you do once and then forget about it. Martin Luther King said it is a "permanent attitude", not an "occasional act". But it's worth the effort.

Forgiveness has a very powerful effect on your life. Holding on to regrets, anger and resentment all have a devastating effect on your body. In my clinic I see clients who cannot

MY BOUNDARY STATEMENT

I will no longer accept ....

....

....

....

....

....

in my life. If this boundary is breached, I will speak
my truth.

Signature: ....

Date: ....

forgive – they are riddled with fears and unhappiness. Not being able to forgive darkens your thought process. How can you think happy and loving thoughts when you have deep forgiveness issues?

Learn to let go and forgive. Now that you have the techniques, you will find it easier to do (see pages 65–6). Not forgiving only draws you into a darkened, fearful life. Learning to forgive is part of your journey, a precious part of the Butterfly Experience. Decide now, here in the safety of the Cocoon stage, to let the pain go. Leave it behind you when you leave this safe place. It will only burden you.

Everything in life is a choice. Make the choices that will set you free to become who you really are. There is perhaps no sadder sight than a butterfly that doesn't have the strength to emerge fully from the chrysalis. Whom do you need to forgive? Write down the person's name and why. There is something powerful about writing down your thoughts – I believe it is one of the most therapeutic ways you can heal. By writing down the impact their actions had on your life, soon you will start to feel free. Write down what you have suffered because of their unkindness. Write down that you are willing to forgive them, because the most important point about this exercise is that you are also forgiving yourself.

Now I want you to complete your Forgiveness Statement.

The next chapter is about a final fabulous Butterfly Experience technique to help you maximize this time of cocooning. Again, it's a technique I want you to use every day.

MY FORGIVENESS STATEMENT

I do hereby forgive ....

for ....

....

....

....

....

Signature: ....

Date: ....

CHAPTER FIFTEEN

Visualization

Manifest your dreams and desires

CHILDREN ARE FANTASTIC because they allow their imagination free rein. They don't judge, don't limit themselves. Now's the time to let *your* head run wild. Think of all the wonderful, positive things you want to accomplish in your life, the places you want to see, the people you want to meet and those you would like to help. Visualization is one of the most important tools available to us.

Visualization is a powerful way to manifest your dreams and desires. It won't cost you any money and it may even manifest money for you. Sounds too good to be true? Most people try to manifest their desires through sheer hard work. But that takes a lot of energy and even then most of us don't achieve all our goals, because we don't use the full capacity of our mind. We keep chasing after our desires as they get farther and farther away. We admire pop stars and actors who have made their dreams come true. How do you think they got to where they are? They had to believe in themselves. What makes them different is the *quality* of their self-belief and their ability to think BIG. They had to know what they wanted.

We don't realize how powerful our minds are until we start using visualization. Through this technique we can manifest anything we want. I'm living proof that by using your thought process you can have *anything*. Today you have the chance to manifest whatever you want, instead of chasing it all your life.

By using this powerful Cocoon tool you will be more in control of your life, you will be happier and your success will be guaranteed. And remember, no matter what age you are, your inner child still yearns for fun and laughter, for adventure. Good visualization includes all these things because a child-like imagination is one of the most powerful resources available to us. If used well, visualization immeasurably enhances our lives.

Remember a time when you wanted something really, really badly – and were sure that you would get it? Think of the effort and action you put into getting it. Think how positive you were about manifesting that item in your life, how you dreamed about it, saw yourself having it. Think how it felt when you finally got it. Remember the euphoria?

Now think of the all times you *didn't believe* you would get something you wanted. What happened then? And how bad did that feel? With visualization you never need to feel that way again! I've used this technique many times to help manifest my dreams, and it will help you to create an abundant life, too.

Visualization

In the Cocoon stage, we use visualization to build on the positive mindset created by the self-relaxation techniques you learned in Chapter Three. And how do we use visualization? By going within. The key to the kingdom, the secret, is within you. Visualization works according to the Law of Attraction (see pages 209–10), but for now it's time for some learning just by doing it!

1. Close your eyes. Use your imagination to put yourself into a picture. It's that simple. For example, think of the sun. Feel its warmth on your skin. Turn the heat up. See its colour. Allow the heat to melt down through your body, gently healing it from head to toe. If you have trouble doing this the first few times, remember that it gets easier with practice, like all the techniques in this book. Just keep on doing it. If you practise often you'll start to feel it, generate it. The mind is truly amazing. Remember that you are in control at all times.

2. Now you understand how to use your imagination, let's apply visualization to your life. First free your mind of any mental clutter. Clear the debris that has gathered there.

3. Start to visualize any situation that you would like to change. Got it? See the situation the way it is now. Now take one aspect of this situation and change it. Turn it into something positive. Here's a simple example. Your car is broken and you can't afford to have it fixed. You would use visualization by seeing yourself sitting in your car, driving around. At this stage you don't need to know

how the car is going to be repaired. You just have to start *believing* it has already been fixed.

4. Each time you do this visualization, change the picture a little more. Focus. Make the image in your head exactly as you want it to be. It may take some time. That's OK. Don't leave out any details. Again, you need to believe in what you are doing, really believe it with all your heart. See the car fixed and yourself driving in it. No matter what, keep focusing on that picture. Let the picture be as colourful and as real as possible. Stay open to Spirit. Remember, the subconscious doesn't know what's true or untrue.

5. Believe it will happen and then wait for the magic. First we manifest in divine mind, then the wonder happens. Before long, help will be on its way. Before you know it, you'll meet a friend who knows a mechanic who owes her a favour. You'll repay him by doing him a good turn. And so the cycle continues.

The five golden rules of visualization

Practise visualization every day. Remember to:

1. **First find your inner calm**. This calm helps you to set your goals in a more directed way. Just by sitting quietly and visualizing an outcome, you are taking steps toward achieving your goals.

2. **Send out wishes in specific form**. Your image must be *exactly* as you want it to be. Remember the old saying, "Be careful what you wish for"? Your imagination is a powerful tool. Use it – visualize the changes you really want to experience.

3. **Meditate on your goals**. Feel what it would be like to have *already achieved* them. What would that look like? What would manifest in your life? Make those ideas as real as possible as you continue to visualize your life improving. Some inspiration, thought or piece of information will jump out. This is your unconscious talking to you. Trust your intuition. Thank it for its gift.

4. **Keep renewing your commitment to your goals**. Write your goals down. Don't worry about how and when they are going to happen. You just need to believe that they will.

5. **Always believe that you can achieve your goals**. Is there any point going for an interview if you only think you *might* get the job? You have to believe that you *will* get it. You have to smell, touch and feel the job. You

have to see yourself in the position, doing the work well, enjoying it. With visualization you will start to believe that you have the job in the bag. When you go along for the interview you'll act as if you have the job. And that self-belief comes across.

Never underestimate the power of visualization. I've used it my whole life. I've waited for the Cocoon stage to explore this wonderful technique because I know that by now your thinking has changed. We visualize because deep down we feel that we deserve good things. At the same time visualization promotes self-belief.

Using visualization to heal the emotions

"I am willing to change"

Feeling lost and searching for something, Aileen was a business owner who had been in a relationship for a long time. She felt that both were going nowhere. Aileen contacted me as she was afraid of change and needed direction in her life. I asked Aileen to describe her vision for her life and helped her to set some goals to start the process. Her goals were to have a new job, a new relationship and a new life.

I taught Aileen how to meditate, visualize and live life with a feeling of love and excitement using the Butterfly Experience techniques and tools. Very soon Aileen had the courage to end her relationship. She also decided to sell her business. Aileen had been living in fear: fear of the future, fear of making decisions, fear of the unknown. She was now able to transform her life and start feeling vibrant, positive, happy and complete. As a result Aileen felt strong enough to make the right decisions and achieved amazing results on both a personal and business level. Every aspect of her life turned around for the better. Very soon Aileen sold the business to her ex-partner, found a new job and found a new relationship. She felt very strong. Aileen continues to use the Butterfly Experience tools and techniques in her daily life.

As this book was going to press, Aileen updated her Butterfly Experience to say:

"My story gets better and better because I have now met the most WONDERFUL man in the whole universe and have never, ever been so happy – ever!!

"Life is good, work is great, work colleagues are brilliant, family are all excellent and new relationship is fabulous."

The magic starts inside, way deep down. Anything can happen if you let it. Why not let the magic happen in your life? You deserve it. YOU ARE SPECIAL.

To give you lots of practice, I've asked you to use visualization in the chapter that follows.

CHAPTER SIXTEEN

Seven Days to a Healthier Relationship with Yourself

Putting it all into practice

Tᴴɪꜱ ᴘʟᴀɴ ᴏꜰꜰᴇʀꜱ some practical suggestions for establishing a better relationship with yourself in just seven days. I give examples of how I embed Butterfly Experience techniques, such as visualization, in my daily life. Each day, try out the suggestions for yourself. When you experience the benefits of putting these techniques into action, you won't want to give them up!

Day One: Enhancing visualization

Make a promise to yourself now to ensure quality sleep for yourself. Establish a gentle unwinding routine that will tell your body you want it to go to sleep soon. Make sure your bed linen is fresh and that your bedroom is a sanctuary – calm and uncluttered. Go to bed at the same time every night, and rise at the same hour every morning.

You will soon have established a rhythm that your body will come to expect. It's important to get plenty of sleep so that the body can recharge itself during the night and be rested for a new day. Unless you allow your body sufficient rest, it will begin to show signs of tiredness, and be lacking in energy. You will experience lethargy and suffer a poor appetite.

For years now I've woken each morning at the same time – 5.00am – by setting my own "head clock". Internationally renowned author Dr Wayne W. Dyer quotes a wonderful phrase from the poet Rumi – "The morning breezes have secrets to tell you." Life is too precious to waste lying in bed.

I begin every day by practising self-relaxation and journaling. Allow 10 to 15 minutes. This is my spiritual discipline and I am faithful to it. This is my time, before the rest of the world wakes up. It's the best part of the day – still and peaceful. I can give my body and mind the time they need.

I spend quiet moments feeding myself the right positive thoughts and giving my body healing. This is when I re-energize, refocus and ground myself for the day ahead.

Discipline is an important part of the visualization techniques I use. I daily reinforce in my mind how I want the day to unfold, planning events and meetings as though they had actually taken place. I make sure to incorporate the things I want to happen, enjoying the positive outcomes I see. Then I give myself three positive affirmations for the day. These are designed to keep me focused and energized.

I dance to wake up and energize my body – usually to the Celine Dion anthem, "I'm Alive". As I dance I celebrate my life, awakening the spirit within me. The physical movement gets the blood circulating round my body. My gratitude helps me to feel bright and awake. Dancing – or any form of exercise, such as yoga or tai chi – raises my vibrations and helps me begin the day with a good level of energy. Without that energy I would struggle to cope with problems that might arise. Finally, I look in the mirror, telling myself that I am strong, healthy and wonderful. I'm now ready for the day ahead.

Day Two: Sharpening hearing

Today we are going to focus on *hearing* within your self-relaxation. I work constantly on heightening my hearing awareness. Paradoxically, I do this by becoming aware of the stillness around me. So few people ever simply sit in silence and just listen. It's a powerful, life-enhancing gift to us. We need silence so that we can listen to the answers our inner knowing will provide.

If this concept is new to you, you may struggle initially to sit in silence. Connection to Spirit is a two-way channel. We talk to our Source. But we must also listen. The secret is to have no expectations, either of yourself or of the Power that is waiting for you to turn to it. Don't be disappointed if you're not immediately enlightened. Be patient. It will come.

Don't allow any distractions. If a thought attempts to intrude, simply acknowledge it, saying to yourself,

"Thinking". If a noise distracts you, say to yourself, "Hearing", and bring yourself back to your inner silence. If your nose starts to itch, don't scratch – the itch will only come back somewhere else. Acknowledge the itch – and let it pass.

When I am still and centred, breathing deeply and regularly, I ask my Higher Self questions, for example: "How can I move on in life?" Sometimes I ask for a sign for ways to fulfil myself today. Or I ask for people to be put in my path – people who will help me move on. At other times the questions are quite specific.

After spending time listening and being, I might use visualization in an auditory sense, to plan things I want to hear that day. For example, I will imagine my coaching practice filled with clients who are achieving wonderful results both in their personal and their business lives.

Another way that we can lift our spirits is through music. Throughout the day I listen to music that I find uplifting. I have always made music part of my life. Music changes how we feel. Music is a vibration. It can lift our mood or it can make us feel sad. When you go to a pop concert, you can feel the energy rising in the hall. Everyone leaves uplifted even though they may have gone along feeling quite low. All their worries have disappeared. Now think of the music troubled teenagers listen to … Research has proven the link between dark, angry music and teenage suicide. Be careful about what you allow yourself to listen to.

Music should be used as a healing experience, or as an energizer (try out the music of Dr Joe Vitale, which is available at www.healingmojomusic.com). Remember that music is played to patients in a coma state to help them wake up! Use this wonderful, symptom-free antidote to life's ills as often as possible. What about other sounds that surround us: people's voices, traffic, the sound of machinery? These, too, can be energizing or draining.

Do not accept any negative words or phrases from anyone. Red-X them out! If someone says something that is untrue or hurtful, you must speak your truth and say so. The person probably doesn't realize that they are hurting you. They may just be lashing out. Hurt people hurt people. So many people are stressed these days that they are sometimes very snappy with others. My response is always to be extra kind to them and thank them for their help. They usually look at me strangely, but they get the point that I'm aware of how they are feeling. Sometimes this is easier to do than to speak your truth.

There can be no hypocrisy here. You're going to have to lead by example. If you speak ill of others, it will be returned to you. Don't get involved in gossip, and learn to compliment people and be kind to others. Make today the day you start using positive language to yourself and others.

Positive self-talk is vital to your health and well-being. If you speak in a positive manner, your vibration rises. You attract a positive outcome back. Would you accept your friend telling you that you look fat and tired? Of course you wouldn't! Then why speak to yourself like that? When you talk to yourself in a positive way your body reacts positively.

Day Three: Heightening the sense of smell

While doing your self-relaxation today, heighten your sense of smell. I created, as part of The Butterfly Experience Collection, the "Pure" Positive Thinking scented candle to help you during your self-relaxation. This wonderful candle with a unique scent will really enhance relaxation (available at www.thebutterflyexperience.com/products). By thinking about the smells around us, of food, perfume, flowers and fruit, we become more aware of them.

Today, spend time in the bath rather than in the shower. Soak in luxuriously scented water. Cleanse your body with a loofah or scrub brush, ridding your body of dead skin cells. Afterwards, massage yourself lovingly with oil, then use scented cream to nourish your body's surface. You don't have to spend lots of money. A few drops of essential oils in base oil such as almond will suffice. The skin is the body's largest organ. Pamper it. It's great to look after yourself, taking care of your body. Our inner child relishes the sense of touch and the scent calms or uplifts us as we require.

Light a scented candle before you do your mirror work today. I remind myself I'm doing this work to help me accept myself as I am. I look at my inner child and ask her how I can improve her life. You can never give too much attention to your inner child. How can you help others if you don't help yourself first?

Day Four: Improving taste

Today you are focusing on new foods. My body has become very sensitive to certain foods – intolerant of wheat. So many foods are made from wheat and my body has been communicating that sensitivity to me over the last few years. I love trying new food sensations and eating healthily. I know that the nourishment I give my body raises my energy vibration. Eating well helps me to stay bright and alert. Eat slowly, relishing the different tastes on your tongue. Make a healthy meal for the family. Treat yourself to a slice of cake or some chocolate. It doesn't need to be your birthday for you to be kind to yourself.

What about food for thought? Spend quiet time. If you enjoy reading, indulge yourself. Each of us has negative thoughts that arise throughout the day. It's how we deal with them that makes the difference. By treating yourself badly, you're also telling other people how to treat you, so it's a self-perpetuating cycle.

I always journal a gratitude list at the end of the day, to thank the universe for the wonderful moments I've experienced and all the abundance I've been given. I thank the universe for the food and shelter that have been mine, for the love in my family. We take such things for granted, but there are so many people in life whose basic needs for comfort and security aren't met. You never know what's around the corner, so be appreciative of life's bounty.

Day Five: Touch awareness

When you get up, look in the mirror and talk to your body in a positive way, telling yourself that you are gorgeous, beautiful, strong, healthy and confident. Who else is going to tell you?

Your 15 minutes of self-relaxation will help you to be more aware of your body. After showering, I smooth on cocoa butter body lotion, repeating the movements over my body slowly and lovingly. I do this to give my body the respect it deserves, and it sets me up with a good attitude for the rest of the day.

Today, choose clothes made from soft fabrics that caress your body. Clothes speak volumes about how you feel about yourself. Do you wear baggy clothes to hide your figure? Do you only wear dark fabrics? Or are you happy with your shape and comfortable in your own skin? Lying to yourself about your size is foolish. Are there clothes in your wardrobe that you haven't been able to wear for years, but can't throw out because of the memories surrounding them? Do you fear that you'll never get back to that size if you throw them away? So many women have a range of sizes in their wardrobe. Don't yo-yo diet. Why not experiment with brightly coloured, fitted clothes that show off your shape? Today, I want you to accept who you are and the size you are. Clear out your wardrobe!

As a fun way of heightening my sense of touch, I enjoy shuffling a pack of playing cards. I look at the colours and the suits then close my eyes and feel the cards. I ask myself to tell me when I am touching a red card by making that colour bright in my mind. I ask for a black card to appear as a dull blackness in my mind. I am *feeling* the colours, seeing the images with my inner eye. This heightens my awareness – try it for yourself.

Make some Butterfly Experience Affirmation cards and plant them around your home in places where you can read them aloud to yourself as the day passes. I find doing this makes me feel happier and more in control. In order to change negative thinking, you first have to be aware of your thoughts.

Day Six: Energy awareness

Today you're going to make a conscious effort to be kind to yourself – to treat yourself the way you would your best friend. Make it the day to celebrate who you are. Buy yourself a treat, such as a bouquet of flowers (one perfect flower is enough if money is tight), then rent a DVD or go out with your friends. Pamper yourself. Tell yourself you love yourself. You have to make yourself *feel* special and soon you'll start to believe it!

Doing self-relaxation every day and raising your vibrations will give you the energy required for a busy life. But today I want you to focus on ways to bring down your energy expenditure. If you are feeling stressed, have a long soak in the bath. I take time each week simply to sit in my garden or a park for 30 minutes, listening to the birds and the wind talk. I heighten my awareness of the world around me, and the energy that flows through it – the plants are energy, the grass under my feet is energy. I ground myself in universal energy, absorb it consciously. By breathing deeply and freely, we can expand our energy vibration. It is such a calming feeling.

Our belongings are all imbued with our energy, and with practice we can all pick up on this. You only have to be open to using all your senses. Try this experiment on Day Six. Ask your friends to sit in a circle. Pass around a few personal possessions, without knowing whom they belong to. Touch them, pick up on their vibration. Close your eyes and ask your Higher Self for any information about that object. You will be surprised at how often your and your friends' "gut instinct" is right.

Day Seven: Tapping into universal energy

Each day, after practising my self-relaxation and raising my vibrations, I spend time sending out positive energy to the world. Not to individuals, but to the universe, knowing that my energy is contributing to making the world a better place. Spend time today researching a spiritual practice that will provide structure and discipline for your life.

Now that you have reached the end of the week, you are on your way to looking and feeling better. You should be looking forward to spending a relaxing day doing whatever you want. Reading that book you've been looking forward to or going to a favourite spot that lifts your spirit. Today is a "do anything day". You choose.

I always make sure that at some point in the week I go for a brisk walk. Exercise stimulates blood flow, as well as burning fat. It keeps your body healthy and makes you feel invigorated. Exercise also counteracts depression, so make sure you do some several times a week. You can join a gym so long as it's something you enjoy, otherwise it will be short-lived. Walking is wonderful exercise and it doesn't cost anything but shoe leather. Think of an activity you've always wanted to do – again, it has to be realistic, achievable. Join a keep-fit group or a salsa class, or learn yoga. Remember the value of exercising with others – it's a great motivator.

This is a day to do whatever you want, and appreciate your life. Enjoy it. Recharge your batteries for a new week ahead. If you're blessed with family, make a conscious decision to enjoy their company. We spend so much time working and so little with our loved ones. MAKE THAT TIME NOW. Mark it in your diary.

Breaking out of the cocoon

We all need support and unconditional acceptance. We find it and give it at home, but there will always be times in life when we need extra strength and extra support – from friends, our Spirit source, from our inner selves. It makes sense to top up our spiritual bank often and generously – so that we have sufficient resources when times are harder.

You have the choice to step out of your comfort zone right NOW and start to live the life you've always dreamed of. An abundant life is not just for other people, it's for you, too. You are part of this world, a part of God. All you have to do is make a decision to claim your birthright.

The last change is often the hardest. You may still feel trapped – the last vestiges of pride and fear may be holding you back. Don't let old thinking get in the way of what you deserve. Sometimes in life we have to ask for help. If that's the way you're feeling, turn now to Spirit and ask for courage. That thought will be picked up as a vibration and help will come. In fact you're already attracting it by sending out positive energy.

You've gone through growing pains, begun to assimilate changes and your persistence is already paying off. Your tool bag is filled with goodies, already overflowing with abundance. There is still a lot to learn. Now that you are feeling more positive and happier about yourself, you can start to create abundance in your life your way. Don't just follow other people blindly. Only you can make the changes that will bring joy, happiness and abundance.

A little faith, a little courage. Can you feel that the cocoon is starting to open? I hope you sense a building urgency and excitement. I want you to harness the energy you're feeling now. Visualization is a tremendous source of power. It will help you to break free of the cocoon that's binding you, so that you can enjoy the life that's waiting for you. Did you know that just before a butterfly breaks free, the chrysalis becomes completely clear? Let's get you there …

Dream big, OK?

It's TIME!

STAGE FOUR · THE BUTTERFLY

Learning to Fly

CHAPTER SEVENTEEN

The Importance of Goals

THE MOMENT WHEN THE butterfly frees itself of its chrysalis and emerges is magical. Treasure it. This is the moment when you finally reject what's wrong in your life – the way your colleague treats you, the conditions you've been living in, perhaps even the abuse you've been a victim of. This is a beautiful moment of Awareness. This is the moment we become aware we are worthy of real love.

Think about all the emotions and healing that have gone into the Butterfly Experience so far, as you have lived the process, refining it all the time. Hasn't it all been worth it? To know what you want from life? More than that – to feel that you deserve it? As you take this first flight feel the magic. You *should* feel thrilled with all you've achieved so far. Enjoy that feeling. Be like the newly emerged butterfly basking in the sunshine, allowing its wings to dry before it flies off to whatever adventures await it.

Spread your wings. You are a miracle of transformation, an ever-changing masterpiece. Commemorate this first bright flight into life's sunshine. I want you to find some way of celebrating your new freedom that's uniquely personal to yourself. And I want you to remember it. Every time you see a butterfly, I want you to say a little prayer of thanks that you found the courage to emerge from your shell – to show the world the Real You.

I love what Primo Levi said about butterflies: "We would not think them so beautiful if they did not fly." It's time to put everything you've learned so far to good use. Remember – this is not a one-off opportunity. The most wonderful aspect of the Butterfly Experience is that you can revisit sections of it time and time again. Retreat into Cocoon if you need to feel safe or to take time out to re-evaluate your life. Go back to Caterpillar if you need more energy. And of course the first stage should be revisited on a regular basis, because the work begins again every day, inside all of us.

We need to be reminded of what we have. You've learned so much going through the Butterfly Experience. Now it's time to start reaping the benefits of all the energy that you've invested.

> *"Just living is not enough," said the butterfly,*
> *"one must have sunshine, freedom and*
> *a little flower."*

HANS CHRISTIAN ANDERSEN (1805–1875)

The Butterfly stage is where you capitalize on what you've learned and begin to benefit from all that hard work. Above all you will use this stage to see how you can adapt your new-found skills to life. Adaptation is the key to survival. It's time to move forward. It's time to create your own opportunities. It's time to fly ...

Breaking free

So, first of all, let me assert my firm belief that the only thing we have to fear is fear itself ...

FRANKLIN D. ROOSEVELT (1882–1945)

If I'd told you at the start of this book that you might be feeling a little fear right now, would you have joined me? I remember hanging on to my mother's skirt, on the first day of school, terrified of what the day would bring. I knew I had to leave her, but I didn't want to. She represented safety, security. Similarly, when we commit to buying our first home we're full of fear. Will we be able to afford it? Will we cope with the responsibility? At this stage of the Butterfly Experience, some of you will experience fear. The thought of staying safe and warm in the cocoon is very appealing. Who knows what's waiting out there?

But change is coming. Why not embrace it, commit to it, be in control as it happens? Otherwise you'll always be accepting second best. Besides – the best is yet to come!

By now you should be feeling calmer and lighter – you've shed so much. As you grow through this process you will understand that the only way out is walking out of your comfort zone and past your fear, allowing yourself to welcome change. Stepping out of your comfort zone – your first, dizzying flight as a butterfly – doesn't have to be nerve-wracking. You just need to think in a different way. Life is open, exciting. One of the most important tools for the emergent butterfly is *awareness*. Knowing what's holding you back and working through those emotions.

Your life up until now has been fairly average or you wouldn't be reading this book. Living as a butterfly means being filled with joy and happiness. It means being free to live your own life. No one can control you anymore, or tell you how you should feel. You are free to live your life any way you want. Yes, you *can* have it all.

My philosophy is you either work with the Laws of the Universe (see pages 209–31) or you work against them. You can struggle and make yourself unwell. Or you can learn acceptance and use the skills that the Butterfly Experience teaches. Life can be easy. Either you are controlling your life or you are out of control. You decide.

When you think as a butterfly you think in a more positive, focused way. Your confidence is raised and your health is improved. You are more in control of your life. You have a sense of purpose. Now take flight. One small, dizzying flight – and then another. Relish the changes.

Congratulations for sticking with me and learning the techniques along the way. That's self-discipline. You are now seeing results on the final stage of your journey. I want to teach you the skill that will really get you to where you want to be in life. I want to teach you …

Goal-setting

Fragile though they are, butterflies have control over their lives. I want the same for you and here's how: *goal-setting*.

Norman Vincent Peale rightly pointed out that all successful people have a goal. But most people are afraid to set goals. They'd rather feel safe and secure in their old patterns and routines. Goals take them too far out of their comfort zone. But goal-setting is what sets successful people apart from the herd. Having goals mean being brave enough to set out all the things you want to achieve. When we set goals we are raising our standards, and giving ourselves a focus and a path to walk.

Setting your goal is as important as achieving it. Once you set your goal, magical things begin to happen. You have sent your wish, your thoughts and your mental images out into the universe. Speak your truth in life. Don't be afraid to tell people what your dreams are.

"Don't put a ceiling on yourself," as Oprah Winfrey says. She is a good example of someone who throughout her life has followed her goal. She believes that affirming what you want is "a message to both you and others about what you think is possible." Today, Oprah uses her radio show as a vehicle for inspirational people to tell their story. Oprah's own life was not always happy. Sexually abused as a child, she comforted herself with food. But Oprah had a goal – she wanted to help others. Overweight, a woman and black, she had a hard road ahead of her, one that would have had most people turning back. But Oprah kept her eye on her goal at all times. Throughout her life she kept focused on the outcome, rather than dwelling on setbacks. An inspiration for social change, Oprah has shown that she has learned to love herself. Now she is teaching others to do the same.

I don't believe in coincidence or in being in the right place at the right time. I believe that we need to make our own luck. I will not accept "No" for an answer and I will not accept second best. How do you get to that place? By setting goals.

Whenever I meet successful people, people who have achieved wonderful things, they invariably tell me it all started with an idea, something that they were striving toward. Everyone has to have a goal in life, something to aspire to. By setting goals we are creating our future.

Goals create our purpose in life.

Goals provide us with a focus.

Goals help us to filter out the unimportant.

Goals help us to overcome our fears.

Goals increase our motivation.

Goals help us to challenge ourselves.

By concentrating all our energy and thoughts we achieve immediate results. The pop-singer Madonna, a woman who's the epitome of success, points out that so many people are scared to say what they want – "That's why they don't get what they want," she says.

Although they involve planning for the future, goals are also about living in the NOW. Goals are not cast in stone. Goals evolve. They're revisited and revised constantly so you can move forward. By setting your goals, you move beyond self-doubt. Goals help you to think in a positive way, which leads to greater success. Success breeds better self-esteem and more confidence. Goals help when you're struggling with circumstances beyond your control.

Everyone has days when things don't go according to plan. Everyone has bad days. It's how you cope with negative experiences that counts. The key is what you do next. For example, less-than-hoped-for exam results should never be seen as a failure. They help you to acknowledge that you've either disliked the subject or not studied for it, or else that you didn't understand the material in the first place. If you admit that you tried your best on the day with the knowledge that you had, you release your inner stress.

Move on to something you *do* like! Set a different goal. Don't let pride force you to keep battling on at something for which you have little aptitude. Know your strengths and work with them.

You need to have the right goal. Are you focusing your energies in the right direction? Don't fall into the trap of having unrealistic dreams. Set yourself small, easy steps that will take you on your way to success. Whether you need to gain a skill, take up further education, re-train or network, set out to learn and grow. We all have to move with the times, so keep up to date with new technology. We don't always need to know how it works. Not everyone who drives a car knows how it works either.

Goal-setting is more scientific that people realize. It has rules. Goals must be:

- **Long term**, in order for you to have a clear focus. (What do you want to do with your life?)

- **Short term**, to show you how to move forward on a daily basis. (What do I have to do today?)

- **Achievable**, so that you can recognize your successes.

- **Flexible**, because life constantly changes and growth attracts new opportunities.

- **Measurable**, so that you can set deadlines.

- **For you**, not for anyone else.

- **Written down**, so that the universe can see them and for you to fully feel them.

- **Given time**, so that they can actually happen.

Here are two great ways to keep your goals achievable!

1. Set S.M.A.R.T. goals

These are goals that are **S**pecific, **M**easurable, **A**ttainable, **R**ealistic and **T**ime-framed:

- **Specific goals**. When we set a specific goal, as opposed to working toward a vague idea, we stay focused. We have to give ourselves clear instructions. Specific goal-setting helps us define more clearly exactly what our goal is. Say you want to lose weight – how much weight do you want to lose? Write it down!

- **Measurable goals**. Let's stay with weight loss. How long will it take you to achieve your goal? How will you know when you've reached it? Will you join a weight-loss class and commit to going each week? Measure your progress steadily and stay on track.

- **Attainable goals**. Goals that are out of your reach will only bring disappointment. There is no point in setting yourself up for goals that are unattainable. You've decided how much weight to lose. Can you meet this target without feeling guilty or unhappy? Most goals are attainable if you set your mind to them and take steps to carry out your plan. Once you have identified your goal, you can begin to look at how you can achieve it. Build some flexibility into your plan, as some things are out of your control. While training for a race, for example, you may develop ill health, which results in a poor performance. A sales representative may work hard, develop strategies and market a product, but if there is an economic decline fewer people may buy it. Be open to achieving your goal in different ways – ways that previously you might have dismissed.

- **Realistic goals**. Goals are achieved by breaking them down, bit by bit. It wouldn't be a goal if everything could be accomplished instantly. Don't try to lose the weight too quickly. We learn and grow as we continue our journey. Breaking goals down gives us the confidence and determination to go on to the next step.

- **Time-framed goals**. Unless you give yourself a deadline, you have no sense of urgency. Without a time frame, you'll get bored and lose interest. You'll have no challenge to rise to. What is your time frame? Weeks? Months? Make sure that your goal is achievable in that time. Do you have a special occasion coming up and want to lose weight beforehand? Then choose to do it, if it's realistic. Set a time frame and stick to it.

2. Ask great questions

Here's another method of goal-setting I've used in my own life to great success. When I decided to branch out and work on my own, establishing my own clinic, I knew I had several decisions to make. So I set myself a series of great questions looking for great answers:

- Why do I want to start working solo?

- Where would I work from?

- What treatment and training would I offer?

- Who could help me achieve my goal?

- When did I want to open my business?

Once I had established these things, and only then, could I start taking action to achieve those goals. Every day I took some action, however small, that would take me a step closer to achieving my goals. Making a phone call, networking, giving talks to raise my profile … every day I achieved something that brought my goals closer.

My time frame was six months, a measurable, achievable time. I knew I could make it happen. Three months before the deadline, I had achieved everything I had set out to do. We must always remember to focus on the outcome. By taking small steps toward our goals, we will achieve our dreams.

> *Obstacles cannot crush me. Every obstacle yields to stern resolve. He who is fixed to a star does not change his mind.*
>
> **LEONARDO DA VINCI (1452–1519)**

You can use the same method. I'm going to use the example of weight loss to illustrate my point. If you want to lose weight, then focus on your goal by asking the following questions:

- WHAT do I want to achieve with my weight?

- WHY do I want to lose weight?

- WHO is going to help me achieve my weight-loss goal?

- WHERE will I go to get help with the weight loss?

- WHEN will I be able to achieve the weight loss by?

Now you know how to set a goal, decide what YOUR goal is! As the American guru of sales technique Tom Hopkins puts it, "You can't rest unless you set goals that make you stretch." Remember I told you that you would find your path in this book? Well, this is where it happens. But first I want to give you a few words of caution: Be careful what you wish for – wishes do come true.

You can choose anything at all from life's menu. Just remember that material goods bring great responsibilities. You only have to look at a random selection of lottery millionaires to realize that money can't buy you happiness. But if you want to attract financial abundance, ask Spirit for something that will manifest money.

JOURNAL: EXERCISE TWELVE

Setting a Goal

Turn to your Butterfly Experience Journal and:

- Write down one goal that you want to achieve

- List the three actions you need to take to reach that goal. Write down who will help you and when you will achieve it.

This is the first step to making your dream a reality!

CHAPTER EIGHTEEN

The Butterfly Experience Seven-step Blueprint

Seven steps to your dreams

Your Butterfly Experience Blueprint draws on all the work you have done through this book so far, so refer to your notes in your Butterfly Experience Journal. This chapter is all about refining your vision, deepening your purpose.

1. What is your vision for your life?

We've talked about why we need goals and how to set them. Now it's crunch time! Time to get off the fence. Time to decide what you want to *do* with your life. Ultimately, your life is going to be on hold until you finally admit what your purpose is, what fulfils you and makes you smile, and what you want your life's legacy to be. Dump all the excuses for inaction that you've come up with so far. You have all the tools you need.

I need you to go to Spirit now and thank its energy for all the blessings in your life to date. Ask Spirit for help in making this powerful, mystical process real. Ask Spirit to give you all the answers you already know, but were too afraid to voice till now.

It's not the outer you that you are changing, it's the inner you – your thoughts, emotions and feelings. When change happens inside, the outside takes care of itself. Something has happened within you already. There is a sparkle, a magic when someone really loves life and is truly happy. The Power is within each and every one of us. Once we unlock the habitual patterns of our thought process, we free ourselves to find the whole new life that is waiting to be lived. Are you ready?

This is *your* life. No one can change it except you. You have the techniques. You're in control, feeling better, thinking in a positive way. Now it's time to take the next step. Really reach out and make those dreams come true. Don't waste your precious life. Look at yourself in the mirror right now and ask yourself: "What do I want?"

It's time to reconsider the wish list that you made in Chapter Four. What do you really want? Do you want …

- A Rolls Royce?

- A new home?

- Good health?

- Happiness?

- The holidays you've always longed for?

- A new challenge?

- New opportunities?

- To help others?

- To give more of yourself?

- To get back into education?

- To leave your dead-end job?

- To improve your relationship?

JOURNAL: EXERCISE THIRTEEN

What You Want to Accomplish

Turn to your Butterfly Experience Journal and:

- Write down all the things that you now want to accomplish in your lifetime.

- Write down when you will start working on them.

The choices are endless.

Still struggling to decide? Here's one of the quickest, most effective ways for finding out *exactly* what you want. Your findings may surprise you.

I'm a very visual person, so I find it quite hard to learn just by reading text. When I was training in clinical hypnosis, I came across Tony Buzan's wonderful books on learning through mind mapping. His ideas intrigued me. The brain thinks primarily from image centres and then radiates out. Walt Disney said of his achievements, "It all started with an image." In other words, our brain works by forming pictures. We remember through imagination and association. For example, if you think of a sunset, your mind will see images and colours, not words. When I am rehearsing a talk, I use certain images to trigger words in my mind. People are amazed to discover I don't speak from notes. It all comes from my heart, from the Power within me.

JOURNAL: EXERCISE FOURTEEN

Create Your Butterfly Experience Mind Map

Something very powerful happens when we commit our dreams to paper. They come alive. You've rewritten your wish list. Use it now to create a map of your life, drawing on Buzan's concept of the mind map. Make your map as bright and exciting as you can. Choose colours and symbols that trigger ideas in you. They should represent the thoughts you want to retain, or symbolize the hidden desires in your subconscious. There are no restrictions – no right or wrong way to do it. Just get on with it!

- Turn to your Butterfly Experience Journal and draw a picture of your home. Sketch how you want it to look. It doesn't matter that you're not Rembrandt.

- Add simple symbols representing those things you want your home to include.

- Now draw paths leading off from your home. You decide where those paths lead – to a new car, happiness, "me time", work, travel, holidays, new skills, relationships ... the list is endless. You're limited only by your imagination.

- Add smaller paths leading off the main ones. Visualize how challenges along the way will lead to new opportunities. Make your journey adventurous, Make it exciting. Make it dangerous. Give yourself opportunities to step out of your comfort zone. You are now controlling your life, so only good can happen. Remember, you created your own fears and anxieties. Here's a chance to control your negative thinking. You can change your perception of challenges – through acceptance, courage and self-relaxation. Make the map as colourful as you want. Make the journey as long or as short as you want it to be.

2. Work on your Self

Now that you know what you want, it's time to acknowledge your Self. What is unique about you? What good qualities do you have that are going to get you where you want to be? How are you going to achieve those dreams? Keep working on yourself, using the self-relaxation and Red-X techniques.

As new issues crop up in your life, divest yourself of negative energies. Remember how it feels to be sandbagged by senseless resentments and feelings of frustration. Work on fear as it raises its ugly head, using the Overcoming Fear visualization (see pages 82–3). Use mirror work (see pages 152–9) to improve your self-esteem.

3. Refine your vision

Use the goal-setting techniques (see pages 191–8) to make your dreams a reality. What steps to you need to take to start? Who can help you achieve your dreams? When do you want to achieve them by? How can you do more of the things you enjoy? Are your dreams realistic and achievable? Choose dreams that you can work toward. And if circumstances change, change your vision. A butterfly will move if it doesn't find what it needs. You need to be flexible, too.

Goals Checklist

From your plan, pick out the short-term goal you know you can achieve first, and put your energy into achieving it by doing the following:

- Write down why you want to achieve that goal. ☐

- Write down how you can help others and yourself by achieving this goal. ☐

- Set yourself a time frame. ☐

- Practise visualization every day along with your self-relaxation to strengthen your vision. What would it feel like to have achieved your goal? How would you look? Where would you be living? What would your friends say? ☐ ➤

- Make that first phone call and get into action. ☐

4. Commit to yourself

Stop making excuses and start today. Think big and take the first steps now. You owe it to yourself. Set a time frame by dating your order to the universe. Give time to what you want to manifest. Trust that when you send your order out to the universe, the energy will begin to work right away. You will start to put the energy into action to make your dreams happen. Commit to being your Highest Self. Use the Three C's from the Caterpillar stage (see pages 91–4) to get you there – Commitment, Courage and Control.

5. Model yourself on successful people

Look at people who have already achieved success and find out how they did it. Seek out a mentor who is willing to share with you how they achieved their goals (for example at www.thebutterflyexperience.com). When the student is ready, the teacher will appear. Don't be afraid to ask for help along the way.

6. Remember that action speaks louder than words

When you take action, you are moving in the direction of your dream. No matter how long it takes, keep focused on your goal. You have to trust that the universe will deliver your order at just the right time – universal time, not our time. Don't keep wondering when your wishes will manifest. When I "ordered" my new home from the universe, many things had to take place before the right one for me came on the market. The important thing to remember is that you are moving one step nearer every day. You don't know when you will achieve your dream. But it will happen sooner if you have enough *desire,* if you *persevere*, if you stay *determined*, if you *trust* it will happen. Before long your order will be delivered. Everything happens in universal time, God's time. We just have to be patient.

7. Have the right attitude

Remember to thank God – or whatever term you use – for all things, for the abundance in your life as well as all the lessons you receive daily. You're about to master the challenges of life as a butterfly. Are you excited? Can you feel the sense of hope and new beginnings?

Now that you know where you're headed, the hard work really begins for the butterfly. Every year as the leaves change and temperatures fall, certain butterflies travel thousands of miles, battling strong winds and flying over perilous landscapes to get to their wintering grounds – dealing with challenges. Even at this stage there are obstacles to overcome.

This stage of the Butterfly Experience is going to show you how to deal with wind and stormy weather – the obstacles and setbacks that we all encounter. Even within the same species and within the same season, every butterfly has its own unique experience of life. The Butterfly stage is going to teach you how to work with the laws of nature, how to exploit the universe's tailwinds, if you like, in order to get the best out of any given situation.

Did you know that the adult butterfly's sight is so good that it can travel over long distances, seeing clearly any dangers in its path? Now more than ever you're going to need a sense of vision. And you're going to need focus.

The importance of focused concentration

Concentration is the secret of strength ...
RALPH WALDO EMERSON (1803–1882)

Focused concentration is the key to success. It is learning to quieten the mind and empty it of clutter. This is hard to do but with practice you will soon find yourself more content, happy and fulfilled. Do it right and you'll be free of stress.

When concentrating on any one thing, avoid tension in the body. Practise concentrating on different objects. Think of mountains far away and then of an object, such as an orange, close to you. Think of small objects and then large objects; see them far away and close by. This will start to train your mind. I often begin by imagining the closed bud of a water lily opening up. I focus on the flower to stop my mind from wandering. Sometimes I see water or colours; sometimes these are near and at other times they're far away.

Practise, practise, practise! By practising self-relaxation daily you are well on your way to learning how to empty your mind of clutter. An empty mind allows you to concentrate on what you are doing. When you meditate, focus on that alone. Similarly, when you are at work, focus totally on the tasks in hand. Don't allow your mind to wander. Bring it constantly back to your subject. It takes time and practice to train the mind, but you'll enjoy real benefits. If you concentrate your mind, your energy will increase. The Dalai Lama says that a person with a busy mind simply needs to meditate for longer.

All that we are is the result of what we have thought.

THE BUDDHA (*c.* 563–*c.* 483 BCE)

Having decided its flight path, the butterfly has several tasks ahead. It needs to take advantage of air currents to ease its journey, avoid predators, seek nourishment and find a mate and reproduce. The challenges that butterflies face are like ours in many ways. How do they meet them? Nature is very wise. Butterflies know how to conserve their strength and avoid predators. Butterflies seek out shaded spots to rest, bask in sunshine to restore their energies, wait in the most advantageous places for the right mate and lay their eggs in protected places. They develop predator-avoidance strategies. In other words, butterflies work with their environment. Similarly, to survive and to be happy in life, wise people take advantage of the Laws of the Universe. You will find out about these in the next chapter …

CHAPTER NINETEEN

The Laws of the Universe

Having an uncluttered mind allows us to focus on what we want. Just like the butterfly searching for nectar, you too can have the best in life. By keeping a positive attitude you will attract opportunities to your life. Did you know that butterflies contain magnetic particles? Just like the butterfly we, too, are magnets – we attract and give off energy. That's because of ...

The Law of Attraction

Like attracts like. Think about your friends, the kinship you share, how their lives run parallel to yours. What we think we attract. That's why we have like-minded partners or friends. The Law of Attraction applies in all circumstances. If you are consciously thinking about something, you will attract that into the physical world. There's a hook to this law – it applies equally to positive and negative manifestations. Don't think about what you don't want or that's what you will create. By giving your thoughts to that energy you will attract it.

If you are feeling low, you attract negative people like a magnet. Your energy attracts someone with the same vibration. The good news is you can easily raise your vibrations by using self-relaxation. Regular daily practice of self-relaxation has astonishing results, helping you to attract a happier partner, more positive friends and more opportunities. As you sow, so you shall reap. What you give out, you get back. Again, it's all about spiritual responsibility. What have you done today to help another person? Did you make life easier for your colleagues by having a positive attitude? Or did you send them running from you with a scowl? A smile costs nothing and goes a long way to healing wounds.

When you think and act in a positive manner, you rid your mind of negativity. Through positive thinking you become free of the ties that bind – anger, resentment, anxiety and guilt – the ties that hold you back from an abundant life. Remember to work constantly at creating positive things in life, and rid yourself of negative thinking every day by using the Red-X Technique (see pages 74–5).

Once you have decided what it is you want to attract, you have to believe that you will receive it *abundantly*.

The Law of Abundance

Reflect upon your present blessings, of which every man has plenty, not on your past misfortunes, of which all men have some.

CHARLES DICKENS (1812–1870)

Now that you've set your goals and refined your vision, I want you to take it to the next level. Imagine what it would be like to create unlimited abundance – health, wealth, prosperity, happiness. How it would feel to have everything you have ever dreamed of? Hold that thought, because I'm going to teach you the principles of abundance. But first, I want you to get a clearer understanding of what abundance means for *you*.

I recently met a successful businessman, a former rally driver, who told me that he had once broken his back in three places as a result of a driving accident. He would have been paralyzed if not for the three steel plates that doctors fitted in his spine. After the accident he faced a long and painful recovery. While he was recovering in hospital, his business suffered badly and his family lost their home. He was too ill to be told. It was only when he came out of hospital that he realized what had happened. In that moment he had a sudden, profound understanding of abundance. Homeless and disabled, he still had what was really important in life – his family. Through sheer determination and hard work he had created a successful business, but his family had suffered. He had been living life literally "in the fast lane" and had forgotten what really mattered. Now he understood how close he had come to losing everything – not just through his accident. Since then he has never forgotten to be grateful for the blessings in his life.

Take a few moments to think about what abundance means to you.

Abundance lies within each and every one of us. It's rooted in our perceptions. We all think if only we had a better job, more money, a shinier car, then we'd be happy. Please know this truth – we cannot achieve true happiness through financial means alone. If we believe that abundance lies outside our physical body, we become stressed and physically ill in the search for it. The source of abundance lies within us.

Abundance isn't about things. Abundance is an attitude. Abundance is not something we can touch, but rather something that we feel deep inside. It's about recognizing and experiencing real joy in our lives. Nothing stays the same, *nothing*. Houses are built and then they get knocked down – just the same as lives. We achieve great things and then something happens and we have to start all over again. The joy is in the building and achieving.

To create abundance, we need to abide by certain universal laws. The butterfly knows that it requires energy-rich nectar to survive, so it goes to where the nectar is found. It doesn't seek aimlessly. When we follow the universal laws, observing their principles, we receive more abundance than we could ever dream of. Most of us are too "busy" to think about universal laws, far less respect them. Ancient wisdom has become lost in our race to get ahead. Most people define abundance as working hard and making a lot of money in order to buy more material goods. As a result many people are overworked and become exhausted. Their bodies can suffer and they can become depressed, stressed and fearful.

Yet all the while, each and every one of us has an unlimited supply of abundance in our life. A South African farmer, with a fertile plot of land and a good living, sold his property to go dig for diamonds. That farmer ended his life in penury. In later years digging work began on his old farm. It unearthed the greatest diamonds the world had ever seen. The company that grew up around this untold wealth was named after the poor farmer who had abandoned his acres of diamonds in search of wealth. The company is known today as De Beers.

I'm urging you today to search for the treasure within. Our sense of self-worth is nowhere more evident than in the limitations of our thinking. You don't have to be a religious person, a spiritual person or even a good person to find the wonders that are waiting within you. Spirit doesn't discriminate. We all have the right to an abundant life, a life filled with happiness, love and fulfilment. But certain rules apply. Am I willing to help others or am I just thinking of myself? What qualities do I want to be remembered for? Can I learn to forgive? Can I learn to let go of resentment and take control of my own life?

When we ask the above questions, something deep within us starts to make us think. We do not have to wheel and deal to create abundance at the expense of others – that could never bring us fulfilment. When we consciously search for the answers to these questions, something shifts internally – we begin to look within for the answers. They might not appear right away. Be patient.

Rules for Affirmations to Create Abundance

When making positive statements for abundance always make sure that:

- Your affirmations are in the present tense.

- Your affirmations are positive.

- You say your affirmations with feeling.

- You say your affirmations each and every day.

Start today and create your Butterfly Experience Abundance Affirmations. Here are some ideas:

I am overflowing with abundance.

Everything I do in life is for the good of mankind.

I am filled with positive energy.

I trust in the process of life.

I am willing to be open to change.

I am truly blessed with abundance.

My spiritual bank account is overflowing with abundance.

I am filled with divine energy and abundance.

If you follow your self-relaxation and positive thinking techniques, you will be able to achieve a higher percentage of abundance each day. Only you can do it.

Make a commitment now to create an abundant life.

Commit to the process every morning, by practising self–relaxation for 15 minutes. Choose a part of your life – for example, health, career or family – in which you want to create abundance. Once you have counted yourself down into your meditative state (see pages 30–32), start creating your new life. Imagine that you already have the abundance you desire. Be aware of what it feels like. Thank the universe for providing this abundance for you. Then your body will act as if your wishes have already come true!

So many people fear that there is not enough abundance to go round. Every morning I mentally go down to the ocean and fill my basket up with whatever I need for that day. There is no need to overfill the basket – I can always return tomorrow. One day I may need energy to see me through a difficult day. Other days I may fill up the basket with new clients. You choose what to fill up your basket with.

My life has been filled with so much abundance. I have three beautiful children – Iain, Jennifer and Calum – who bring me happiness every day of my life. I have a fabulous husband: Gordon is my rock. My mother and father taught me to be strong and always to think big and believe I could achieve anything. I've had the friendship, love and support of a wonderful sister, Rosemary, and her family. I have the gift of friendship and have built an amazing team of people who are always ready to help. I have my health and am truly blessed with a wonderful gift of being able to help and heal others. This is my dream. I'm living it and I thank God every day for the abundance in my life.

The key to abundance

There is an old story of a king who visits a subject in jail, promising him his freedom. The prisoner waits for many years, but the king does not return. Finally in desperation and on the verge of suicide, the prisoner goes to the cell door to beg to be released. He finds the door unlocked.

Some of us are imprisoned in a prison of our own making. We have erected the bars and they consist only of fear. You have the power to set yourself free, to recreate your life. Love yourself, love others – this isn't a cliché or a theory. It's the key to an abundant, spiritual life. When you act and think this way, you send out a different message to the universe, and it repays you in kind. The Buddhists understand this – it's all about compassion. And it has to start with yourself.

You're not what you think you are. But what you think, you are! Look seriously at your life. Take time. Reflect on the past. Look at your daily behaviour, evaluate it honestly. Then ask yourself: "How much abundance am I creating?" and "How many acts of kindness have I performed today?" Small deeds add up – together they create a happy life. Every day we add to this spiritual bank account, the abundance just keeps on multiplying. We give away and then we receive. Begin to understand the spirit of this fundamental law, and see how it *transforms your life from the inside out.*

A loss of a butterfly species in an area tells scientists that there is something wrong with the habitat. What emotional habitat are you giving to your dreams and your desires? Are you sabotaging your ability to manifest abundance? Remember your belief system buried in your subconscious. What is it telling you? Do any of these ideas strike a chord with you?:

- Money is the root of all evil.

- Money doesn't bring happiness.

- Money is scarce.

- Money goes to others.

- Money slips through my fingers.

Whatever you've been programmed to think about money, you can change it. Money is not the problem – our attitude to it causes problems.

A client shared his story with me recently. He had just been made redundant, had no money and was in debt. He went into his office and prayed fervently, holding on to his faith that something would change. Twenty minutes later he received a phone call offering him a job. He asked me if this was a coincidence. My response? "There is no such thing as coincidence." My source of funding is simple: God is my source.

That said, I credit myself with the ability to make the abundance I desire become real. The converse also applies. How often do we hear about people winning the lottery and then losing it, ending back at square one within a short time? Those people simply don't believe that they deserve financial abundance.

The philosophy of enough

Before we think about how to create financial abundance, let's look at this from a different perspective, to get you thinking. I'd like to talk about the philosophy of enough. We all need money to live on, its energy to survive. But exactly how *much* money do we need? Most people's problems are rooted in this question. How much of their anxiety about money is actually self-inflicted? People worry unnecessarily, feeling that they must have the latest status symbol in order to feel good about themselves. But we all know that today's huge, wide-screen television is tomorrow's debt. Wanting causes stress and stress leads to illness.

Have you ever really thought about how you choose to spend your money? Some people choose to spend extravagant amounts on socializing, trying to drink their way to happiness. Some go on luxury holidays and buy fast cars or houses they can barely afford. Most households today require two incomes – two parents working outside the home, just to make ends meet. But what if all the unnecessary items we buy were taken out of the agenda? How much of our income do we spend on clothes and other material goods to add to the façade of what we hope people think we are? It's a self-perpetuating nightmare of consumerism – once we buy into it, it's extremely difficult to fight our way back to sanity. What are we trying to prove to ourselves? People try to divest themselves of stress with strenuous workouts. Why spend money going to the latest class at the gym in an effort to ease your stress? Keep your money in your pocket. Practise your self-relaxation for 15 minutes each day and you'll soon see the difference this crucial time makes.

> *A man's life consisteth not in the abundance of things which he possesseth.*
>
> **THE BIBLE, LUKE 12:15**

It would be great if we got everything we asked for in life. If every desire, every goal, every wish came true, we would be so happy. Or would we? What would happen to our sense of purpose then? There would be no striving. No sense of achievement after struggling to make something happen. Think of the hard work involved when you save for a holiday. The satisfaction you get from reaching your goal, the fun and that special feeling of being on holiday. Would it feel as good if you could have it all the time?

Without struggle you would be unable to grow spiritually and mentally. Life would be boring. If God allowed us to go through life without any difficulties, we would be paralyzed by apathy. We need obstacles in order to learn and grow.

A newly minted lottery winner thought that all his problems were solved when he won the money. Instead he came to realize that he had replaced his old difficulties with a whole new set of problems. Money is difficult for so many people. It causes dissension and bad feeling even among people who love each other. Hence the sayings, "Money is a curse", and "Money is the root of all evil". The latter one is actually a misquote – the Bible says that the *love* of money is the root of all evil, a very subtle, very powerful difference. We dread being without money. Financial insecurity, perceived or real, makes us grasping and fearful. By thinking "Me, me, me!" and always taking from life, we reinforce our fear, the feelings that we are not secure and not worthy.

The Law of Abundance tells us to act entirely differently. It tells us that when we give to the world, the universe rewards us. And the negative also applies – if we give out nothing, we receive nothing back. When I spent time listening to the Dalai Lama, I was struck by his message that our path in life must be for the benefit of all. How can we enjoy wealth if we are surrounded by poverty? How can we achieve great things if we know we are hurting our fellow human beings?

Give what you can without thought of reciprocity – that way everything is a blessing. The great philanthropists of the world, such as Andrew Carnegie and, in more recent times, Bill Gates, know that money is simply energy. We can't try to keep it to ourselves, especially when there is so much need in the world

I have long understood this principle and seen it working in my life. As a result I have had many abundant rewards. Any time I have needed money to pay an unexpected bill, or to do something I really wanted that would enhance my spiritual well-being, I've received a letter or a phone call – a company asking me to give a training course, perhaps, or more clients booking in.

If this principle has worked for me, it will work for you. Ask for ways in which you can create abundance –

a promotion at work, a new job or a new contract for your business. In turn these will improve your finances. There is enough, more than enough for everyone. We only have to be open to one action: helping others.

Another name for the Law of Abundance is the Law of Manifestation. If you believe in your right to abundance, then you will create it. *You deserve it.*

When you start to understand that abundance is within each and every one of us, you can start to sow the seeds to create an abundant life. When you set a clear intention, when you believe you deserve abundance, it manifests itself. Do you believe you deserve to be happy, wealthy and successful? If not, why not? What you believe, you create.

We miss out on so many opportunities in life by being negative. There will be times when we feel low, angry or sad, but we need to remember that *we* are causing those emotions through our negative thinking. We sometimes feel that life has dealt us a terrible blow, and can't understand the lesson we are meant to draw from it. But if we wait, believing that in time more will be revealed, more *will* be revealed. There is a whole big world waiting for us. We just have to connect to Spirit.

Louise L. Hay is a wonderful spiritual teacher who has created an abundant flow of wealth for herself and helped thousands of people all over the world. When Louise receives a bill through the post, she writes her cheque and sends it back with love and kindness. She says the company sent it knowing she could pay. What a wonderful attitude to have! Why don't you pay your next bill with love and openness, grateful that you can afford to do so? And if you are struggling to pay, try believing that the universe will provide what you need in some way and use that energy to seek a solution, rather than use the same energy worrying.

If only everyone could have this mindset, our universe would be a different place. Change has to start somewhere, so let it start with you. Just watch and see what happens. We all have daily choices to make that help us lead the kind of life we want. Some people take the easy option and just allow life to pass them by. Others become angry and bitter, causing damage to themselves and those around them. But others choose joy, choose love. When we choose this path we know we are working with universal law. Joy and peace enter your life, unlike anything you've experienced before. When you start to help others, something inside changes. Something magical happens when you reach out to other people. You are no longer alone. Choosing right thought and right action gives you the energy to do more. You become calmer, more confident and more attractive to be around.

The Law of Vibration

Now that you're working on attracting abundance, you need to make sure you stay on track. Even within the world of butterflies, different species have different approaches to their life journey. What is your approach to be? That will depend on the Law of Vibration.

The Law of Vibration is that something vibrating at a certain frequency will resonate with and attract things vibrating at the same frequency. Our thoughts and feelings are all energy and vibration. Music is vibration, words are vibration. Thought transference works on the Law of Vibration – when we think thoughts and send them out to the universe, they are picked up on the same vibration. Have you ever wondered why you sometimes think about a friend and then the phone rings and it's your friend, who's also been thinking about you? It's no coincidence. Thoughts transfer. We often say that someone is "on the same wavelength" as we are – that means they're on the same vibration. You automatically feel comfortable with that person, you speak the same language.

Your thoughts and feelings determine your vibration, which in turn determines who and what you attract. By really understanding this you can attract so much more abundance into your life. Reading through this book has already triggered thoughts and feelings that allow you to attract the right energy to complete this work.

Be on the lookout for the physical signs – tension, tightness – which precede negative situations. They act almost like a magnet, drawing the negative to us. Heed the message from your subconscious and avoid anything that makes you feel like that.

Prayer is vibration. When we send a prayer, we are sending a spiritual connection. The universe is always waiting. As soon as we connect to universal energy, we immediately feel that energy vibrating around us. But unless we ask we won't get.

Be aware that negative thought vibrations can subconsciously sabotage your wish list to the universe. Always be vigilant against negative thoughts. Be your own spiritual detective. Avoid negative vibrations as much as possible – those depressing TV programmes and newspaper headlines. Feed yourself only positive information. Be on your guard and never let it down. When you are on your authentic path, life events vibrate with you – you know instinctively if they are right or wrong for you.

The Law of Cause and Effect

This is the law that states: "Do unto others as you would have them do unto you." There can be few more ancient disciplines than the law of karma. As you grow in spirit, you begin to see the link between your thoughts, your actions and your reality. Any emotional discomfort or pain you experience is associated with cause and effect.

If we are suffering it is because we have a karmic lesson to learn. Many people fool themselves, thinking that they can get away with hurting someone, but the universe always remembers. We will be forced to learn our lesson at some point. No one escapes this cosmic law. Everything you do in life happens because you made it happen. Acknowledging that allows us to learn necessary lessons.

The Law of Gratitude

The Law of Gratitude is for me one of the most important laws. I believe that it is about having an attitude of gratitude, being grateful in life for everything, no matter how small.

We have so many blessings. It is important to remember that not everyone has them. So many people focus on what they don't have and forget what they do have. Be grateful for what you have.

Gratitude never fails. Possibly more than any other attitude in life, being grateful will help your progress. It is important to thank the universe for all you have. We have to be thankful for our health, our homes, our food and our families. Are you grateful for the simple things: the grass, the blue sky, the ocean, the flowers, the animals, the air that you breathe? Do you love your work for the job satisfaction and the material blessings it brings? If you're at home, are you grateful for the roof over your head and for the time you have with your children?

We have to be grateful in all circumstances. This life is a learning process, which allows you to expand. A Chinese folk tale demonstrates this principle. There was once a poor farmer, who possessed only one horse. When the horse ran away, all his neighbours felt sorry for him, but the farmer merely shrugged, refusing to rant and rail at the gods. The following day the horse returned, bringing with it a herd of wild horses straight into the farmer's coral. His neighbours rejoiced and the farmer gave thanks. The next day his son was breaking in one of the horses and fell and broke his leg. All their neighbours said the horses were cursed; the farmer merely shrugged his shoulders. A week later, the Chinese army swept through the village, taking with it every young man fit to fight. The farmer's son, with his broken leg, was left behind. And the farmer gave thanks, because he understood …

The Law of Love

The American inventor and politician Benjamin Franklin (1706–1790) expressed this law well: "If you would be loved, love and be lovable." A life without love is no life at all. Love is the foundation of our life. The love you have for your partner, the love you have for a newborn baby, the love you have for yourself. Love is all around us. Some people choose to love animals, or the world they live in. Without love we perish.

Motivational guru Anthony Robbins is a prime example of this lesson. Someone helping him as a young man made a lasting impression on his life. He made his mind up at that moment that he would serve others. But he did this out of a sense of love for them – not to cover his ego in glory. We don't all have his resources, but we can have his willingness. If everyone did one thing every day to help someone else, the world would be a better place. When we start to help others we are helping ourselves. When we give to others the universe gives to us.

For our spiritual well-being, it is vital to consider what we can do to help others. Don't know where to start? Try smiling at someone you don't know. Reaching out to someone can really make a difference. As Mother Teresa pointed out, sometimes the worst poverty is loneliness and the feeling of being unwanted. Maybe the stranger will look slightly bemused, but nine times out of ten they will return your smile. Just think how good that person will feel and it will make you feel good, too. Don't delay your happiness. There is a whole new life waiting for you. Start today.

Learning to accept people for who they are is a life skill – we can work at it. Human beings, like butterflies, come in lots of different varieties. Some are aggressive, others are placid. Some are shy, others are confident. Some are rude and arrogant, others are kind. Learning how to cope with all types of people is important. More important is learning to stand up for ourselves and being able to say "No".

So many people enjoy being the victim. Dealing with negative people can be very draining and it is vital that we protect ourselves from them. Don't be afraid to make a break with people I refer to as "energy vampires". If someone is sapping you of strength, it's better to end the relationship in as kind a way as possible. Just make sure they aren't reflecting your own energy!

I had a client who came to see me with confidence issues. When we dug deeper into her story I discovered that she had a relationship problem – with herself and her colleagues. They all "ignored" her and as a result she didn't like them. I asked her why they didn't talk to her. She replied, "Perhaps it's because I don't speak to them."

If we are unhappy with ourselves, we see ourselves reflected back in others. Her colleagues were a mirror image of her own insecurities. I asked her to smile at every person in the office every day for the rest of the week. The following week she had to go a step farther – smile and say hello. By the end of the first week a colleague had asked her out to lunch. They realized as they talked that they had a lot in common. Mirror images of each other, you might say.

If we are dishonest we think others are, too. If we gossip, we presume others talk about us, too. When we get entangled with other people's negative talk it rubs off on us. It is negative energy. What you give out you get back, so be careful what you say. Remember words are vibrations. They reach other people. It's a better use of that energy to send kind thoughts to someone who's unwell.

People struggle with the idea that "If you can spot it you've got it." But a little honesty, a little humility will take us a long way here. Are you ready to put your hand up to the truth?

I want you to think of someone you don't feel comfortable around. Ask yourself why. What is it about them that you don't like? Now ask yourself whether you have any of those traits. Chances are the things you don't like in others are the same things you don't like about yourself.

But there may be a reason why you feel you can't love someone. The Law of Love does not require you to love you friends and family unconditionally. Take a minute to think about who your friends are. Do they reflect you – or do you deserve better? On your journey as a butterfly you may come in contact with predators disguised as friends. People who make nice comments to your face, but talk about you behind your back. People who take advantage when you're feeling vulnerable. People who steal your ideas, your money, your time. If the conditions around butterflies become unacceptable they have to decide whether to stay put or whether to go. When you change yourself, the relationships you have with others change, too. We seek in friendships our own values, boundaries and principles. On no account must you lower your standards.

It's very important to keep yourself grounded. I love to

walk in nature – trees are full of positive energy. I often hug a tree to ground myself. People may laugh but it helps me get rid of other people's negative thoughts and feelings. Avoid predators at all costs, especially if they try to knock your confidence. What is missing from their lives? Use them as an example of who you don't want to be.

Romantic relationships

Soon after it emerges, the butterfly is ready to find a mate in order to reproduce. But mating can be a hazardous process for a butterfly, so take care! Don't be blinded by the wrong mate's beauty. It's easy to be dazzled by the array of colours and patterns out there. Butterflies, however, assess their mates on grounds of *health* and *willingness*. There's a lesson for us there. Is the person you're with, or interested in, emotionally and spiritually well? If not, give them a wide berth until they've done their own healing. Is your partner willing to commit? Is your partner emotionally and spiritually available?

Everyone has a signature scent, transmitted via chemicals called pheromones. Male butterflies give out chemical signals to other butterflies – territory control signals to males, attraction signals to females. But how do pheromones work for humans? We also detect pheromone molecules, inside the cavity of the nose. The information is transmitted to the hypothalamus, the area in the brain that controls emotions and sexual activity.

Interdependence means being dependent on others for some needs. We have to work on our relationship with our

Self in order to have a healthy relationship with another person. If we believe only this person, this pet or this material possession will make us happy, we become a victim. Some butterflies fly in tandem, locked together. This is dangerous for both butterflies – they're vulnerable to predators because their movements and vision are limited. Is this happening in your relationship?

Male butterflies are very selective in choosing a female partner. Just like a person looking for the strongest, healthiest, best-looking mate, the male butterfly is always looking out for the most attractive females. But some people seek out the weakest people so that they can dominate them, trying to control their partner's lives.

Co-dependence means taking care of others at the expense of yourself. Does this ring bells with you? Co-dependency leads to feelings of guilt, feelings that you can never do enough, working too much, depression, feelings of isolation, perfectionism, having no clear boundaries, low self-esteem, constantly looking for approval from others, being unable to take any responsibility for your own actions. Sound familiar? Then maybe it's time to make that relationship with yourself now before you can start any other relationship. We tend to fall back on co-dependent relationships because of a fear of being independent and of standing alone.

Healthy romantic relationships should be neither interdependent nor co-dependent. It's also vital when starting a new relationship to set boundaries.

You need to work at your relationships. There is no magic wand. Whether it's a relationship with a friend, your partner, your husband or your wife, the same principle applies. There is no such thing as living happily ever after, unless you invest in the relationship.

Lessons will be repeated until they are learned

We learn lessons from the day we are born. We never stop learning. Like the gentle unfolding of each butterfly, all our lives contain mysteries that won't be known until the last page is complete.

Life is a wonderful journey. We all have opportunities to achieve what we want. Yet while some seize those chances with both hands, wringing every bit of joy out of life, others take longer to learn life's lessons. They insist on doing things their way, instead of aligning themselves with the universe and its laws. Sometimes this has drastic consequences – people end up in prison, or damaged in some way that denies their freedom.

Remember: until we learn our lessons we will need to keep repeating them! Until I learned that, I used to please others. Until I took responsibility for who I am and learned to say "No", life was much harder. My health suffered. Saying "No" is difficult to begin with. But I can assure you – with practice it gets easier.

And don't feel that you always have to make decisions straightaway – butterflies, if conditions aren't right, go into *diapause*, a mini-hibernation, to conserve their energy levels. Take your time if a decision is important. If life gets particularly difficult, if the processes that sustain you are threatened somehow, you can find a sunlit, wind-protected clearing and go into a restful period of waiting until conditions are right again.

Butterflies need a safe place to hibernate over winter, to rest from their migratory flights – a warm place to bask in the sunshine, to soak up the sun's energy. I know that if you use the Butterfly Experience techniques, you too can find such a place in your life. A place to rest, within yourself. A place that makes you feel comfortable. Forget about keeping up with the Joneses. Make a home for yourself that is a safe harbour from life's storms. We all need that sense of belonging.

Learn from the best. Never pass up an opportunity to add to your store of knowledge. And don't ignore the wisdom of the people around you. I learned many lessons from both my father and my mother. They taught me to appreciate the good things in life and all that I had. My grandfather taught me self-discipline. Lessons like these are essential to our growth. But we cannot grow unless we learn to live in the now.

CHAPTER TWENTY

Live in the Now

TODAY IT'S TIME TO enjoy – to bask in the sunshine like the butterfly you are! Just for today live with joy, hope and happiness. Your fears are only illusions. Tomorrow is another day and you can start all over again.

Too many of us spend our lives thinking of the past. Enjoy the NOW. Stop worrying about what has passed. Take life's experiences and learn from them. Remember the good and process the difficult times. Mulling over unhappy experiences stops you living in the NOW. Think of it as driving a car, constantly looking in the rear-view mirror. How are we to relish life's magic or be aware of positive experiences if we are holding on to the past? Clinging on to traumas and sadness just creates more stress.

The biggest culprit here is the ego. When you make the shift from seeing only the negative in others you begin to see the good in yourself. By letting go, you release the negative and all the stress that goes with it. Change your thoughts!

Accept only quality thinking. Make a point of using your mind to drive you forward in life and help you to be successful. It's about being willing. Are you ready to let go of your negative thoughts and really start a new way of life?

Did you know that a butterfly's wings are much larger than is necessary for flight – they are designed for joy. So choose joy. Choose to be happy right now, this moment. When you live in the NOW you focus only on what you are doing at this present time. Set your goals but remember to live for the NOW. It's the only healthy attitude that you can have. It's good to remember the good times, but don't hold on to negative memories. The difficult times should be left in the past. They are just that. Past. Learn from them. Don't repeat the mistakes. Remember that when you hold all that stress, tension, bitterness and anger inside, it doesn't escape. Its effects will show up in your health at some stage of your life.

Living a "good" life

The world is beautiful. But we are often too caught up in the minutiae of life to fully appreciate its blessings. Too busy to stop and think of others, or ask how we could help keep our planet safe. The media constantly bombards us with images of airbrushed superstars with their airbrushed lifestyles. The subtext of course is that this is how *we* are meant to look, how we are meant to live our lives.

With so much emphasis on the material, who has time to think about who they really are, about expanding their spiritual life, rather than wondering what they need to *have*? Newspaper headlines scream about sports celebrities' earnings. A few days later we see full-page spreads of their partners spending thousands in a single shopping trip. Why does no one see the obscenity of it? Think of the good that money could do in the Third World. We are all guilty of excess to one degree or another. Why do we need possessions to make us feel good about ourselves? The same tabloid headlines show us that money, fame and power are not always the route to peace of mind. Here in the West our basic survival needs are met. Yet we are more dissatisfied and unfulfilled than at any time. Our easy lives have bred selfishness. How often do you stop to think about where the world is heading? Or about your part in improving it?

How many of us take time to really consider our lives? What has happened to the idea that each and every one of us is unique and important? That the differences between us should be cherished and respected? What about our health – our physical, mental and spiritual well-being? Why do we disrespect ourselves the way we do? Why do we reject who we are? Many women pay thousands to look like clones of each other. Plastic surgery is now an everyday event. But it only changes the "you" the world sees. The only person who can change you – the *real* you, the one who wakes up at four o'clock in the morning, heart thumping – is YOU.

So few people seem to have the inner resources to rise above difficulties and cope with what life throws at them. We allow our negative thoughts to grow, allowing them to cause us discomfort. What coping skills are we teaching our young people? In our culture today, it is widely accepted

– almost expected – that the young will binge drink. Nightclubs are full of strangers, unable to speak to each other, flaunting their sexuality in primitive pre-mating rituals that would make cave men shudder in embarrassment. The rise in knife and gun crimes reflects a generation out of control. Why do so many of our young people choose to drink and drug themselves into unconsciousness on a regular basis? Why is no one showing them a better way forward, a simple method they can use to control their lives? Why is no one teaching them the importance of a relationship with a Greater Reality?

Universal energy

For me, a right relationship with myself begins with aligning with the Source of All. The world is made up of billions of different people, with different temperaments, different skin colours and different cultures. Yet we are all one in the world. We come from the same matter. We are all born of the same energy. All over the world we are unified by the experience of praying to some kind of higher power or universal energy. If we tune into this energy, we all get the same results. Why wait for times of fear, anxiety and hopelessness to look to some greater energy for help? I have witnessed so many wonderful events over the years that I have no doubt about whether the universal energy exists.

When I have asked for help in life, help has always come. In times of darkness there is always light. But we are sometimes so blinkered by our obsession with the material world that we fail to see it. No matter what has happened in our lives, it is never too late to begin again, to right our relationship or deepen our understanding of this Wonder.

A client came to me to stop smoking. His body language told me that he was not ready to stop; he was extremely stressed. I advised him to keep his money and come back when he was ready, knowing that he would return. He asked if I had time to speak with him, and whether I had a faith. "It doesn't matter what I believe," I said. "Tell me your story." Falteringly he began, saying he had recently been released from prison where he was being held after committing a terrible crime.

Though not religious, he had been praying for help, holding on to his faith that someone would look after him. Awaiting sentencing, lying in his cell and staring at the wall, he had seen an image of Jesus appear. He heard a voice saying, "I'm going to let you go." He looked around. There was no one there.

When he looked back at the image, a picture of himself had appeared on the wall.

The next day he appeared in court for sentencing. The judge said there was insufficient evidence and he was released. Real faith comes to us in unexpected ways. If we seek it …

We are all energy. Deep within each and every one of us lies a beautiful spirit. Some people commit terrible crimes in life and they live with that knowledge for ever. They have separated themselves from Spirit. We are not born bad or unloved. We create that person. And we can *change* who we are. If you could walk away with one lesson from this book, my wish would be this; that today you learn to take those blinkers off. That you see the light, become conscious of the energy that is just waiting to help you. Let today be a new dawn. Start to build a relationship with yourself, with your inner self, your God Self. Go within and find the cosmic force, the universal life energy that is your birthright. Whatever you call it, *use* it to help you in life. It never fails us.

When we slow down, and begin to listen to the still small voice inside ourselves we realize that Spirit is present in all aspects of our lives. Present in the here and now, present in all we do, present in the people that we meet and in the situations we find ourselves in. Time and time again people get an inkling of what abundance is available to them. But unless you work at it, seek it out on a daily basis, what you experience won't be enough to really help you. You can't stockpile abundance for the future. It has to be of the moment, found in the now.

Spirit gives us messages in so many different ways. We may speak to someone who gives us the information we need. We may hear a song on the radio and a word jumps out. Universal energy works in so many different ways. Dreams are important, too, so take notice of them. I always keep a notebook and pen beside my bed to write down any thoughts or words that come to me on awakening. Spirit comes to us in messages, spiritual postcards almost, in the form of intuition, gut feelings, insights or intuitive thoughts. By developing our awareness of these signs, and more importantly following them on a daily basis, we empower ourselves, aligning ourselves to Spirit, to the Laws of the Universe.

The ego comes up with all manner of excuses as to why we shouldn't believe that universal energy is helping us in this way. Feeling threatened, it will justify any behaviour so long as it stops you going inside. It will allow you to devote time to overeating, binge drinking, watching TV. But it baulks when you want to find 15 minutes to tune into the power that will turn your life around. The ego covets the flash car and the stylish lifestyle, but it won't let you invest time in starting your day right and organizing your priorities.

Take this time to count your blessings and develop an attitude of gratitude for the blessings the day will bring. It all starts inside of you. You are the only one who can create your ideal life. You alone have the power within you. Anything else is a false dependence.

Life goes on

How do I know that Spirit is real? Three months before my father's death, I had a vision. I awoke one night and saw the date and place of his death, and all the family at his funeral. I kept the details to myself but wrote them down. I knew I had been given this vision in order to be strong for my family. When the time came I prepared myself spiritually. I warned my office that I wouldn't be in, that I would be with my father in hospital.

My parents' house was closer to another hospital, but I knew he wouldn't be there. My mother phoned to say that Dad had slipped into a coma and was being taken to a hospital farther afield. I made my way calmly to the hospital as

I knew from my vision that I would have enough time to say goodbye. When I arrived at the hospital, Dad was in bed number seven, a number that I had clearly seen in my revelation and written down. We sat with my father for some time. Around 4.10am, a nurse saw changes in his body, and warned that it was time. I knew from my vision that Dad would pass just after 5.30am. At exactly 5.30 he opened his eyes and looked down at the bottom of his bed. There I saw my father's spirit, as a young man with dark hair, wearing a white, short-sleeved shirt. Several days later I described the moment to my mum. She told me of a photograph I had never seen, showing Dad just as I had described him.

I always ask Spirit for proof and I have never ever been let down. Exactly 10 years later I was given a reading by a well-known medium. He spoke of all that had happened at my father's bedside. He also told me that my father thanked me for giving him a kiss on the forehead before I left. He said that my father knew everything that was going on around him – he had felt his hand being squeezed and knew that one person was not able to make it to the hospital that night.

It is the proof that we all seek: life does go on after death. I most certainly know it does, but not as we might think. Our subconscious awareness goes on. On the morning Dad died, I went home and wrote a eulogy for his funeral, naming the hymns I had been given in my vision. I discovered Dad had chosen those same hymns with my mother a few days before he died. At the funeral everyone wore exactly the outfits I had seen in my vision.

Life moved on. Believing I had to stay strong, I didn't allow myself to grieve my father's passing properly. It was a year before I really went through the process. In the year it took me to realize how badly I was hurting myself, I didn't see any clients who had been bereaved. After I began to grieve properly, my books were full of clients stuck in grief. The universe knows what we can cope with.

It was such a comfort to know that my father's spirit went on. I have great faith in the universe, which helped me get through, to accept finally that my wonderful father was gone. I knew that if I was grateful for my time with him, if I held on to all he had taught me and all the happy memories, he was only a thought away.

Be open to Spirit. You have nothing to fear. We don't need to understand how it works; we just have to believe it does. Trying to understand will accomplish nothing – intellectualizing the process will only slow you down. To get past any doubts you must simply have faith.

CHAPTER TWENTY-ONE

Faith

'If ye have faith … nothing shall be impossible unto you.
THE BIBLE, MATTHEW 17:20

I BELIEVE THAT DEEP DOWN in all of us there is a fundamental yearning to be connected with the Great Source.
We all have desperate moments in our lives – when we are
facing an operation, when we've lost our job – and it's then
that we all need to ask for help. It's said that there are no
atheists in foxholes.

On my journey I have studied and compared many different religions. It's my belief that we all pray to the one
energy. Faith in that energy is the basis of all miracles. But
faith is also a state of mind. To those of us who have it, it is
a *decision*. Faith is knowing that, no matter what, things will
work out, that you are being taken care of, that when you
find yourself in a moment of darkness, there will always be
a light that shines.

I used faith when I enrolled on my clinical hypnotherapy
course, knowing that I didn't have enough money to pay for

the training. Due to acute carpal tunnel syndrome, I had no job and no money coming in. Faith allowed me to take action, believing that Spirit would provide. Within three months of starting my training I had been given a scholarship. All my fees were paid.

Faith allows us to take chances, to welcome opportunities that we would otherwise walk away from. Faith works, at all times and in all circumstances. The great leaders of this world hold on to their own faith, and they never need it more than in times of disaster. An example was the Asian tsunami of 2005. How quickly lives changed. At times like that we question why these things happen and how we should respond. Without faith in a Higher Intelligence we have nothing. Events like that make us stronger people, pull us together, make us revaluate our principles and beliefs and reassess what's important in life. How important is our petty grudge when someone else's world is falling apart? We're trying to be top dog at another person's expense, then the TV screen shows us someone starving and dying. Time for a reality check.

Martin Luther King pointed out that faith is something you take one step at a time, without having "to see the whole staircase". Remember that you already exercise faith every day of your life, without realizing it. When you drive your car down a steep hill, you have absolute faith in the brakes working. When you phone your friends or family abroad, you have faith that the phone will connect you. When you go to the doctor, you have faith that you will be given the right medication. People are too busy thinking that faith means religion to notice that they already have it, all the time.

I also know what it feels like to fall victim to debilitating fear, gut-wrenching anxiety, temporary loss of hope and waning faith. I've had challenges in my own life, worries that I thought had no solution. But in my hour of need, when I feared all was lost, I always kept my faith. It was the light that showed me the way and pulled me back to my self-belief.

I understand the challenges that people face in life. I, too, have had them and continue to have them. It's how we react to those challenges that shapes us.

Just know that no matter what is going on in your life, by holding on to your faith in God, Allah, Our Creator, Spirit – the energy that you believe in, no matter what you call it – good changes will happen. From darkness comes light.

> *Faith is not something to grasp, it is a state to grow into.*
>
> MAHATMA GANDHI (1869–1948)

Every day new lives are begun. Every day couples commit to each other in love and begin their life journey together. Life is what we make it. Life is for living. Through all that I have experienced and learned, I have grown to be a very positive person who loves life. Without my faith I would have found life impossible. When we ask for help, help will come.

The world is constantly changing and right now it is going through great transformation. There has never been a better time to have faith. It will give you the courage to keep moving forward, to form wonderful relationships, to start a fabulous business or simply to live a life with meaning and confidence.

*If a man wishes to be sure of the road he treads on,
he must close his eyes and walk in the dark.*

ST JOHN OF THE CROSS (1542–1591)

We all come from the same Source. I call it God, purely because of the way I feel when I think or say the word. I am not a religious person in a conventional sense, but I do believe there is an energy far greater than man's. When we do our self-relaxation we connect with the divine presence within each and every one of us. I am in touch with my energy every day. I consult my pure energy, my intuition, and listen to the answers it gives me.

By sharing this energy we can really help each other. Divine energy is ignored, disregarded, wasted every day. So many people aren't conscious of the divine energy within them. The divine energy within me triggered me to write this book. I remain grateful to Spirit for the energy I have been given, for my healing abilities. I am in touch with them on a daily basis – I feel energy that others may only be vaguely aware of. That energy allows me to help others.

Abundance for me is the God within. It is all that which my contact with God permits me to do and experience. When you are aligned with your God energy, abundance flows through every level of your existence. We know when we are without it – we struggle and everything seems to go wrong. The self-relaxation and visualization exercises that I offer are not alternatives to conventional prayer, which is an entirely different experience. These are tools to help you to access the life you deserve, to develop the same ability that I have, to tune into that Power.

What used to be passed down from generation to generation has to come now from a new source of knowledge. The seekers among us have rediscovered ancient channels to the Source. We've learned that it's not enough just to accept or reject the dogma given to us by others. We have to experiment with our spirituality until we find out what works for us. We have to look for inspiration from wise men and women who have gone before us.

As life progresses we have to move closer to the energy that creates us, otherwise we'll yearn for it always. But like a marriage, our relationship with the Source requires constant maintenance. It's too easy just to walk away. When we instil discipline in our life and set goals and strive to achieve them, life becomes so much more easy and fulfilling.

Positive thinking at root means having faith and belief in this benign power. By connecting to it we flourish. There will always be the sceptics who need proof. For those of you who remain sceptical, the most inclusive thing I can say is, "Just try it – what have you got to lose?"

For 30 days open yourself up to Spirit. Take 15 minutes for self-relaxation, morning or evening, to allow Spirit in. It's only by experiencing Spirit that you'll know it to be true. Wherever you are, whatever you are doing, it's already inside you.

Believing in miracles

I have much to be grateful for in my own life. I am daily shown wonderful miracles, and that for me is abundance. It gives me a great sense of comfort and peace knowing that I am part of Spirit. I learned to "let go" long ago and, when I did, my life opened up. No more trying. Just *doing*. Working with my clients, helping them to create their new lives, new partnerships, new careers, new friends, helping them to win at life – all of these are miracles. I thank Spirit every day for the opportunities that I have to do my work.

CONGRATULATIONS! You, too, have achieved your goal. You've finished the *Butterfly Experience*. You're ready to put all the lessons into practice as you journey toward your abundant life. You can re-read any section at your leisure. This book has given you tools and techniques that you can use for the rest of your life.

No one would ever deny the butterfly its right to exist. Allow yourself that same right – the right to exist, to be perfect just as you are. Live in the moment. Seize every opportunity. Your new life is waiting. Change today and you will change for ever. I have asked my God that all who read *The Butterfly Experience* be touched by the hand of their God. I wish you all as much fun, laughter and joy on your journey as I've had. My journey goes on – miracles have happened in my own life and continue to, as they will in yours. Wonderful things are happening in my life. Today I have the courage to grab those chances with both hands.

Be strong, have faith and live your life like the butterfly. Make the Butterfly Experience a part of your life every day and God will see you through.

CELEBRATE – THIS IS THE BEGINNING OF
A WONDERFUL NEW LIFE!

The Butterfly Experience Journal

EXERCISE ONE
Your Butterfly Experience Affirmations (page 37)
Choose up to three areas in your life that you would most
like to enhance. For example, money, career and weight.
Write one Butterfly Experience Affirmation for each area.

Butterfly Experience Affirmations:

....

....

....

Write down how you would feel if these things were
already manifest in your life.

....

....

....

EXERCISE TWO
What Makes You Happy? (page 38)
Write down three things that make you happy. For
example, meeting a friend, going on holiday or watching
a good movie.

....

....

....

Write down three actions you need to take to make
you happy.

....

....

....

EXERCISE THREE
What Would Improve Your Life? (pages 39–40)
Write down seven things in your life that need changing.
Don't miss anything out. Really think about what you want
out of life. Say these things out loud and notice how your
body reacts.

....

....

....

....

....

....

....

Write down the area in your life that you most need to change, and three actions you can take to improve it.

....

....

....

EXERCISE FOUR

Count Your Blessings (pages 40–41)

Write down the things that your life has been blessed with – create a gratitude list.

....

....

....

Write down three things you are good at.

....

....

....

EXERCISE FIVE

What Do You Really Want in Life? (pages 42–3)

Write down all the things you desire in your life – your wish list. Don't leave anything out.

I desire ....

....

....

Write down three actions you need to take to achieve
these things.

....

....

....

Now write down the things you wanted to do and have in
your life, and that you regret not doing.

....

....

....

Write down three actions you need to take to start
achieving them.

....

....

....

I am willing to be open to change

Signature: ....

Date: ....

EXERCISE SIX
Create the Life You Deserve (page 44)
Write down a list of your best qualities.

....

....

....

Write down three actions you need to take to improve
your life.

....

....

....

EXERCISE SEVEN
What's Good About You? (page 44–5)
Write down seven positive thoughts about yourself.
It's OK to repeat qualities from Exercise Six.

....

....

....

....

....

....

....

EXERCISE EIGHT
Back to Basics (page 46)
Write down Butterfly Experience Affirmations for each of the seven categories you wanted to change in Exercise Three. For example, career, family, relationships and finance.

....

....

....

....

....

....

....

EXERCISE NINE
What is Success? (pages 134–5)
Write down what you consider success to be. What are all the things that you think make people successful? What makes you feel successful?

....

....

....

Write down three actions to improve your success.

....

....

....

EXERCISE TEN
Gratitude (page 148)
Look over your gratitude list (Exercise Four) and add three more non-materialistic things you are grateful for.

....

....

....

EXERCISE ELEVEN
Mirror Work (page 156)
Have a good look at yourself in the mirror. Write down all the good things you notice about your appearance – your warm smile, for example.

....

....

....

Now write down three things you need to do to improve your image. For example, apply make-up or have a haircut.

....

....

....

EXERCISE TWELVE
Setting a Goal (page 198)
Write down one goal that you want to achieve

....

Write down three actions you need to take to achieve that goal. Who will help you and when will you achieve it?

....

....

....

EXERCISE THIRTEEN
What You Want to Accomplish (page 201)
Write down all the things you now want to accomplish.

....

....

....

When are you going to start working on them?

....

....

....

EXERCISE FOURTEEN
Create Your Butterfly Experience Mind Map
(pages 202–3)
Use your wish and future accomplishment lists to draw your mind map overleaf. Draw a picture of your home in the centre of your page, and continue with paths leading to a new car, a new career, different goals, holidays, places that you want to see. You decide. Make it as exciting as you want your life to be.

YOUR BUTTERFLY EXPERIENCE MIND MAP

Useful Websites

Karen Whitelaw-Smith
www.thebutterflyexperience.com

Dr Joe Vitale
www.mrfire.com
www.healingmojomusic.com

Karen King and Salma Fomradas
www.unboundedpotential.com

Kim Kelley Thompson
www.kimkelleyproductions.com

Bob Proctor
www.bobproctor.com

Tony Robbins
www.tonyrobbins.com

Esther Hicks
www.abraham-hicks.com

Jack Canfield
www.jackcanfield.com

Triumphant Events
www.triumphantevents.co.uk

Gordon R. Smith
www.instarhr.com

Debora J. Hollick
www.insightfulsolutions.com

Joyce McKee
www.letstalktradeshows.com

Crown Talent
www.crowntalent.co.uk

Stevie Vann Lange
www.stevielange.com

British Society
of Clinical Hypnosis
www.bsch.org.uk

Recommended Reading

Richard Branson, *Business Stripped Bare*, Virgin Books: London, 2008

Norman Doidge, *The Brain That Changes Itself*, Viking Penguin: New York, 2007

Dr Wayne W. Dyer, *The Power of Intention*, Hay House: Carlsbad, 2004

Louise L. Hay, *You Can Heal Your Life*, Hay House: Carlsbad, 2004 (new edition)

Napoleon Hill, *Think and Grow Rich*, Capston Publishing: Chichester, 2009 (new edition)

Napoleon Hill and W. Clement Stone, *Success Through A Positive Mental Attitude*, Thorsons: London, 1990 (new edition)

Mother Teresa, *A Simple Path*, Ballantine Books: London, 1995

Norman Vincent Peale, *The Power of Positive Thinking*, Simon and Schuster: New York, 2003 (new edition)

Robert A. Russell, *God Works Through Faith*, DeVorss & Company: Los Angeles, 1957
—— *You Too Can Be Prosperous*, DeVorss & Company: Los Angeles, 2000 (revised edition)

Robin Sharma, *The Monk Who Sold His Ferrari*, Harper Collins: London, 2004

Bernie S. Siegel, *Love, Medicine and Miracles*, Random House: London, 1999 (new edition)

Joe Vitale, *The Attractor Factor*, John Wiley & Sons: Hoboken, 2008
—— *Blue Healer* (audio CD, available from www.healingmojomusic.com)
—— *Instant Manifestation*, Portable Empire: Wimberley, 2011
—— *Strut* (audio CD, available from www.getupandstrut.com)

Wallace D. Wattles, *The Science of Getting Rich*, Destiny Books: Vermont, 2007 (reprint)

Paramahansa Yogananda, *Autobiography of a Yogi*, Self Realization Fellowship: Los Angeles, 2006 (new edition)